ESSENTIAL ASSEMBLIES FOR ALL

Vol. I

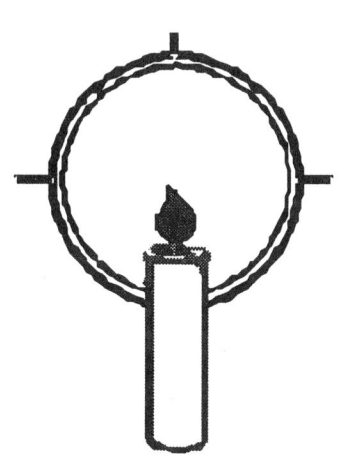

CLARUS PUBLICATIONS

51 Kader Avenue, Acklam, Middlesbrough, Cleveland TS5 8NH

Vin Shanley
February 1996

FOREWORD

The Teacher who is responsible for an Assembly needs to have suitable material which is readily available, and can be turned to and used *without first having to spend hours on its preparation*. The presentation of an Assembly is never an easy task because, not only is it daunting for anyone to have to perform before colleagues, but in addition, the ingredients which are used have to be suitably meaningful and interesting to their intended audience. The Assembly provides the Teacher with an added dimension in larger-group communication, offering a unique opportunity for sharing a message with a significant section of the School in circumstances which are tranquil and when a major impact can be made.

To help in that process, this volume, the first in a series, has been specifically structured to incorporate features which, experience has shown, are ideally suited to encourage *Christian aspirations and ideals,* and to nurture the appropriate *positive values,* in a stimulating, lively and entertaining way. Every Assembly in this file conforms to a consistent, user-friendly, format *(i.e. Main Text, Materials for O.H.P., Resources Summary)* which includes the following:

- **An Introduction:** To set the scene for the **THEME** of the Assembly.

- **Story/Stories:** These **EXPLAIN** the theme in an effective, meaningful and exciting way. Everybody enjoys a "good story", and those included here have been selected from real situations to convey the relevant messages.

- **Photographs/Cartoons/Diagrams, etc.:** These **ILLUSTRATE** the theme and the stories. The lay-out is such that they can be copied directly on to acetate sheets for O.H.P. to provide visual impact which will help clarify and vitalise the whole presentation.

- **Readings:** Relevant **SCRIPTURE READINGS** and/or **PRAYERS** help to provide a focus for corporate reflection.

- **Music:** A selection of appropriate **RECORDINGS** of popular songs, from the '60s to the present day, provides a suitable aural stimulus, based on the theme for each Assembly.

- **A Conclusion:** This brings everything together and **REINFORCES THE CENTRAL MESSAGE** of the Assembly.

A VARIETY OF METHODS OF DELIVERY

The attraction of this collection is that each self-contained module is so structured that every Assembly, as outlined above, provides the Teacher with the flexibility of using a variety of strategies in its presentation. The Teacher can opt to be the sole presenter throughout, or the Pupils themselves can easily deliver all or any of the components. For example, the Teacher may wish to introduce and conclude the Assembly while Pupils read the stories, manage the O.H.Ps., read out the scripture passage and explain the significance of the music.

Everything is included here for a complete and effective Assembly, with or without reference to additional material. However, where time constraints so dictate, any one theme lends itself readily to be extended over 2-3 successive Assemblies, without any loss of continuity, by extracting from the module as many, or as few, elements at any one time, as may suit the immediate purposes of the presenter. There is also ample scope for the presenter to "personalise" the presentation, by incorporating any additional material which is more directly relevant to his or her audience.

The O.H.P. material is presented in composite form, but is also cross-referenced in the main text in order to optimise its impact within the context of the Assembly.

These are Assemblies which will take the toil out of preparation, which you will enjoy delivering, and which, using only an overhead projector and a cassette player, will enable you to present a worthwhile and valuable message to your Pupils and Students.

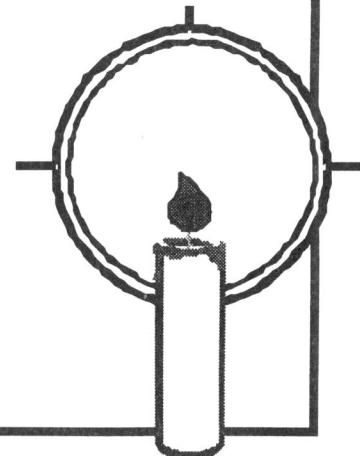

Vin Shanley
February 1996

CONTENTS

1 School Values and Pupil Targets
2 School - A Place to Work Together
3 Surviving and Coping at School: 1
4 Surviving and Coping at School: 2
5 Potential
6 Remembrance Day
7 Passing Tests: 1
8 Passing Tests: 2
9 Causes of Trouble at Home
10 Is the Grass Really Greener ...?
11 The Best Interpretation
12 The Tragedy of Rejection
13 The Human Will and Spirit
14 Young People: Do Times Really Change?
15 Peace
16 The Sadness and the Hope of Death
17 Famine
18 Talk and Gossip
19 A New Start
20 Care on Holiday

SCHOOL VALUES AND PUPIL TARGETS

INTRODUCTION ...

Teachers have a profound influence upon their charges, and in our modern society they are the ones who, for the most part, are providing the moral and social, as well as the academic, direction which has been surrendered by so many parents, and which the churches are having difficulty in supplying since, for the most part, they have failed to obtain access to youngsters.

Pupils should be reminded regularly of what the school stands for, and the moral values which it embraces and supports and the philosophies and conduct which it rejects. The **additional burden** for Teachers is to set out clearly how pupils might progress academically and socially to enhance their educational prospects and live useful and contented lives within the community.

VALUES

Each institution is unique and will have an emphasis on different values depending on all sorts of extraneous circumstances. Here is a suggested sample ...

TARGETS

Targets set will depend upon each particular year group as well as each individual. However, there are basic objectives which pupils throughout their schooling might strive to attain.

O.H.P. 3

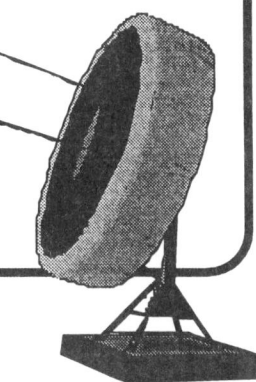

SCHOOL VALUES AND PUPIL TARGETS

QUALITIES WHICH WOULD HELP TO ACHIEVE THE TARGETS SET ...

CONFIDENCE IN OWN ABILITIES

When it is seen what some people have achieved with far less capabilities and opportunities than the majority, then it should inspire us all with confidence.

Helen Keller, for example, was born in America in 1880, and after a serious illness when she was eighteen months old, became blind and deaf. Worse was to follow a few months later, when she became mute - she was unable to speak.

Fortunately for Helen, at the age of 6, she came into contact with a remarkable teacher called Anne Sullivan, who herself was partially blind.

Anne taught Helen to read and write Braille, and, painstakingly, how to speak. She taught her so well that, at the age of 24, Helen obtained a first class degree from Radcliffe College in the United States. She went on to write books and travel the World, giving lectures.

It is an astonishing story of someone who achieved so much with so many disabilities.

PERSEVERANCE

It is easy, in the first full flush of determination and exuberance, to say you are going to do something, but it is another matter when you have to keep it going day after day. To give you an example of real perseverance, there is the remarkable story of Don Guixing, who lives in Shanghai.

In a land where the art of the miniature is commonplace - where you can find the Lord's Prayer written on a grain of rice and a boat with its cargo carved out of a plum stone, Don decided that he would master the technique of painting portraits on human hair. It took him two years to prepare for the task:

- So that his hand would be rock steady, each day he held for a few minutes an 8lb. weight at arm's length on a long stick.

- He followed a strict fitness programme and did breathing exercises to lower his heart beat so that it would not cause movement in his hands while painting. He reduced his heart rate to 22 at rest. (Normal heart rate is 75-85.)

- After much trial and error, he discovered that only the whisker of a mouse could be used as a brush.

- It took him a year to find the correct paint.

You can buy one of his portraits for £5,000.

SCHOOL VALUES AND PUPIL TARGETS

QUALITIES WHICH WOULD HELP TO ACHIEVE THE TARGETS SET *(CONTINUED) ...*

HARD WORK

Another necessary ingredient to achieve targets is hard work. No matter how clever or talented someone is, they will not achieve anything of note if they are not prepared to make the required effort.

One man who was regarded as a genius was Michelangelo. He lived in Italy from 1475 until 1565, and was regarded as the greatest artist and sculptor of his day. One of his most famous works is the **PIETA**, a sculpture of Mary, Jesus' mother, holding Him after He had been taken down from the Cross. It took him many years to complete, and you would never realise it, but ...

`O.H.P. 4`

- Mary looks clearly younger than Jesus.
- His body is much smaller than hers, and if she were to stand up, she would be seven feet tall.
- - Yet their faces are the same size.

To arrange the sculpture as he has is clearly the work of someone with outstanding talent, as the rest of his works are, yet this is what he said:

> "If people knew how hard I had to work to gain my mastery, it would not seem wonderful at all."

INDEPENDENCE

Pupils should value, and be encouraged to learn, independence, and not to be influenced by those friends or colleagues who do little themselves and do not want others to do much. Pupils are with their school "friends" for only a few years, but might have 60 years or more to regret their influence.

David Frost once told the story of how he hailed a taxi after emerging from the television studios, and while he was sitting in the back of the cab, the taxi driver reminded him that he had been in the same class as David Frost in the Junior school. David Frost did remember him when he gave his name, and recalled that he had bullied him from the first day he had arrived at the school. He had not impinged upon David Frost's mind for decades, and he took some satisfaction in that his one-time tormentor was ferrying him around and now was so chatty and matey. School years pass like the blink of an eye.

SCHOOL VALUES AND PUPIL TARGETS

SCRIPTURE READING
St. Matthew, Chapter 5: verses 4-10

- Happy are those who mourn;
  God will comfort them.
- Happy are those who are humble;
  They will receive what God has promised.
- Happy are those whose greatest desire is to do what God requires;
  God will satisfy them fully.
- Happy are those who are merciful to others;
  God will be merciful to them.
- Happy are the pure in heart;
  They will see God.
- Happy are those who work for peace;
  God will call them His children.
- Happy are those who are persecuted because they do what God requires;
  The Kingdom of Heaven belongs to them.

ALTERNATIVE READINGS
St. Luke, Chapter 16: verse 10

Whoever is faithful in small matters will be faithful in large ones; whoever is dishonest in small matters will be dishonest in large ones.

Ephesians, Chapter 5: verses 15-17

So be careful how you live. Don't live like ignorant people, but like wise people. Make good use of every opportunity you have, because these are evil days. Don't be fools then, but try and find out what the Lord wants you to do.

SCHOOL VALUES AND PUPIL TARGETS
MATERIAL FOR O.H.P.

O.H.P. 1

VALUES

- RESPECT FOR THE DIGNITY OF THE INDIVIDUAL - rights, feelings, property
- HELPING AND CARING FOR THOSE WEAKER THAN OURSELVES
- THE BEST INTERPRETATION OF THE ACTIONS OF OTHERS
- FORGIVENESS
- TELLING THE TRUTH
- KEEPING PROMISES
- LOYALTY TO FRIENDS
- TAKING PERSONAL RESPONSIBILITY FOR ONE'S ACTIONS
- SELF-DISCIPLINE
- TOLERANCE

O.H.P. 2

VALUES THE SCHOOL WOULD REJECT ...

- BULLYING
- CHEATING
- DECEIT
- CRUELTY
- IRRESPONSIBILITY
- DISHONESTY
- PREJUDICE
- DISCRIMINATION

SCHOOL VALUES AND PUPIL TARGETS

MATERIAL FOR O.H.P.
(Continued)

O.H.P. 3

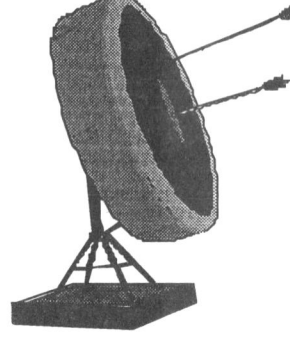

TARGETS

- PUNCTUALITY
- ATTENDANCE
- CO-OPERATION
- TOLERANCE
- GOOD BEHAVIOUR
- CONCENTRATION IN CLASS
- HOMEWORK
- WORKING TOWARDS EXAMS

O.H.P. 4

MICHELANGELO'S "PIETA"

SCHOOL VALUES AND PUPIL TARGETS

SUGGESTED RESOURCES ...

THE PICTURES
(OVERHEAD PROJECTOR)

- Values
- Values the School would reject
- Targets
- The Pieta

THE MUSIC

- "Oh, Very Young" - Cat Stevens
- "Nowhere Man" - The Beatles
- "I Wanna Be A Winner" - Brown Sauce
- "Making Your Mind Up" - Bucks Fizz
- "Ebony and Ivory" - Stevie Wonder and Paul McCartney
- "You Can Get It If You Really Want" - Desmond Dekker
- "I Can See Clearly Now" - Johnny Nash
- "Jesus Christ (Standing Room Only)" - Harvey Andrews
- "Johnny Can't Read" - Don Henley

THE WORDS

SCRIPTURE READING
St. Matthew, Chapter 5: verses 4-10

ALTERNATIVE READINGS
St. Luke, Chapter 16: verse 10
Ephesians, Chapter 5: verses 15-17

SCHOOL - A PLACE TO WORK TOGETHER

INTRODUCTION ...

There is no doubt that education is a very serious business but it does have its lighter side. Here are some true stories connected with school life and learning.

O.H.Ps. 1 - 4

*From the **Daily Express** ...*

"Corned beef was sent to a Bridgend school kitchen. Teachers sniffed it and did not like it. A canteen manageress sniffed it, and said it was good; the town sanitary inspector sniffed it, and he passed it as good; the town medical officer sniffed it and declared it good - then ordered it to be destroyed because too many people had sniffed it."

*From an **R.E. Exam** ...*

Question: Who is the Devil?
Answer: I don't believe in the Devil. It's like Santa Claus - it's your Dad all the time.

*From an **English Exam** ...*

Question: Use "unaware" in a sentence.
Answer: "Unaware" means your vest and your pants.

*Letter from a **Parent to the Headteacher** ...*

"Please don't give our Sally any cabbage for her dinner - she hates it and I have to clean it all out of her socks where she shoves it."

Besides providing the opportunity for you to have a laugh from time to time, school can teach you to obtain many talents - e.g. to read, write, add up, pass exams, speak another language and even boil an egg. However, more important than any of these is that school is a place where you learn to get on with other people, co-operate and develop the right attitude and relationships.

SCHOOL - A PLACE TO WORK TOGETHER

TWO STORIES ABOUT PEOPLE GETTING ON TOGETHER

Story 1: The Heaven of Korea

There is an ancient Korean story which tells of a man who died and was taken on a tour of Hell. He was escorted down beautiful, long and carpeted corridors with expensive paintings and gold-framed mirrors hanging on the walls. Eventually he arrived at a spacious hall in which the tables were weighed down with mouth-watering foods of every description. However, the air was full of shrieking, moaning and ear-piercing screams and shouts of anger and frustration. He watched, covering his ears against the hideous noise, and he saw the cause of the bedlam - the men and women sitting at the tables were struggling to feed themselves, holding the handles of knives and forks which were five feet long. No matter how hard they tried, they could not manage to get the food into their mouths.

He was then taken for a tour of Heaven. He walked down the same type of corridors and came to a similar hall as the one he had seen in Hell. Again there was food of every description on the tables. The difference was that there the people were happy and smiling. Immediately he saw the reason for this. Those eating were using the five feet forks to gather up the food and feed one another. Everyone ate what they wanted, thanks to the help provided by their neighbour.

Story 2: Billy and Jack   O.H.P. 5

There were two great friends who both came from the same beautiful village of Annfield Plain, in North West Durham, and who went off to join the Durham Light Infantry as volunteers when the First World War broke out in 1914. In 1916 they were involved in the bloodiest battle of the war - the Battle of the Somme in North West France. On the third day of the battle, the two of them were seriously injured by a shell which exploded close to them as they were advancing towards the heavily fortified German trenches. They ended up in a crater while the battle raged around them.

Billy had been blinded by the blast while Jack had lost the use of his legs. Six hours after the battle finished, they could hear, in the far distance, the troops moving out. They had been passed over in the frantic search. Billy could not see, but could walk; while Jack could see, but could not walk. So it was that Jack climbed onto Billy's shoulders and in this way they managed to survive the Battle of the Somme.

If, then, people are prepared to work together, share problems and co-operate great things can be achieved.

SCHOOL - A PLACE TO WORK TOGETHER

A CARING COMMUNITY

If individuals wish to belong to a 'caring' community - and the school *is* a community - then they must accept the responsibilities which go with that membership. The basic commitment is an appreciation that each individual is different with his or her own likes, dislikes, strengths and weaknesses, and this fact must be acknowledged.

> ***Men are born equal but they are also born different.***
> (Erich Fromm)

Members lose the respect accorded when they harm or damage someone. In return for the respect members of the community extend to each other, they themselves have a right to enjoy that same consideration and esteem.

This 'caring' aspect is marked in a number of ways. It is displayed in the absence of hurtful, sarcastic and vicious comments. We are also aware that often it is not **what** is said, but **how** it is said which causes distress. Furthermore, psychologists claim that non-verbal communication affects us more than the spoken word and as such we should ask ourselves **how** we speak to others. Do we have a tendency to shout? Do we answer the telephone in a polite manner, or does our tone make it clear we resent having make the effort? Do we listen to what someone is saying to us, or are we just ticking over, waiting for the chance to butt in and say our bit? Do we fit into the category of those who do not listen to a joke or a funny story, but mentally search desperately for a funnier one? Worse still, do our actions while someone is speaking indicate what we are really thinking - do we frown, look aghast, roll our eyes, turn our backs, scratch our heads or look from side to side?

CONCLUSION O.H.P. 6

If school is to be the happiest time of our lives, then it depends upon everyone within the institution showing consideration, tolerance and understanding for the feelings of others. It is through our treatment of others that we shall be happy and learn at school those things that will benefit us in later life.

SCHOOL - A PLACE TO WORK TOGETHER

SCRIPTURE READING
Romans, Chapter 14: verses 8 and 9

Be under obligation to no-one - the only obligation you have is to love one another. Whoever does this has obeyed the Law. The Commandments - "Do not commit adultery; do not steal; do not desire what belongs to someone else" - all these, and any others besides, are summed up in the one Commandment: "Love your neighbour as you love yourself."

ALTERNATIVE READING
Colossians, Chapter 3: verses 12-14

You are the people of God; He loved you and chose you for His own. So, then, you must clothe yourselves with compassion, kindness, humility, gentleness, and patience. Be tolerant with one another and forgive one another whenever any of you has a complaint against someone else. You must forgive one another just as the Lord has forgiven you. And to all these qualities add love, which binds all things together in perfect unity.

SCHOOL - A PLACE TO WORK TOGETHER
MATERIAL FOR O.H.P.

O.H.Ps. 1 - 4

From the "Daily Express"...

"Corned beef was sent to a Bridgend school kitchen. Teachers sniffed it and did not like it. A canteen manageress sniffed it, and said it was good; the town sanitary inspector sniffed it, and he passed it as good; the town medical officer sniffed it and declared it good - then ordered it to be destroyed because too many people had sniffed it."

From an R.E. Examination ...

Question: Who is the Devil?
Answer: I don't believe in the Devil. It's like Santa Claus – it's your Dad all the time.

From an English Examination ...

Question: Use "unaware" in a sentence.
Answer: "Unaware" means your vest and your pants.

Letter from a Parent to the Headteacher ...

"Please don't give our Sally any cabbage for her dinner - she hates it and I have to clean it all out of her socks where she shoves it."

O.H.P. 5

Harmony and Co-operation in School

SCHOOL - A PLACE TO WORK TOGETHER

MATERIAL FOR O.H.P.
(Continued)

O.H.P. 6

Soldiers going "Over the Top": World War I

SCHOOL - A PLACE TO WORK TOGETHER

SUGGESTED RESOURCES ...

THE PICTURES
(OVERHEAD PROJECTOR)

- Quotes from Newspapers, Exam Papers, Notices, etc.
- Harmony and Co-operation in School
- Soldiers going "Over the Top"

THE MUSIC

- "We All Stand Together" - Paul McCartney
- "One Vision" - Queen
- "We Are The Champions" - Queen
- "Old School Yard" - Cat Stevens
- "Let's Work Together" - Canned Heat
- "He Ain't Heavy (He's My Brother)" - The Hollies

THE WORDS

SCRIPTURE READING
Romans, Chapter 14: verses 8 and 9

ALTERNATIVE READING
Colossians, Chapter 3: verses 12-14

SURVIVING AND COPING AT SCHOOL: 1

INTRODUCTION ...

The mass of men wish to live their lives with the minimum of conflict and hassle in a friendly, caring atmosphere where there is kindness, tolerance and forgiveness. The reality, however, is that, where people come together at School or at Work, pressures, tensions and conflicts, at some time or another, do emerge. In our Schools, while we must strive for the ideal, and long for lives in which there is only peace and tranquility, pupils need to be aware of the realities of life. They can count on others to help them in their bid to survive and cope, but they need to know what they are up against and what they can expect. To be forewarned is to be forearmed, and an awareness of the problems which might arise, assists youngsters to realise that the difficulties they will experience are not unique and insurmountable.

ONE STORY OF SURVIVAL : THE AVALANCHE   O.H.P. 1

About nine years ago, in a small village near the Austrian city of Innsbruck, which lies at the foot of the Alps, there lived a young farmer who was called Jacob Jorgenson. His Father owned the farm which, amongst other animals, had a herd of chamois, which were very special because they had been brought in from the Picos de Europa in North-Western Spain. One Saturday night in January, Jacob went with his mates to the local night club where he boogied the night away. When he set out to return home in the early hours of the morning, at about 3 o'clock in the morning, a blizzard, which was particularly severe for that time of the year, was raging. He decided to stay up, have some coffee and breakfast, and at first light, put his skis on and go up to the high pastures just to make sure that the herd of precious chamois was safe. The snow was still falling heavily as he made his way up into the high mountains.

As he climbed higher and higher, the weather grew worse and worse. Suddenly he heard a great roar and recognised the sound immediately. It was the sound of an avalanche, and he realised that it was coming his way. He braced himself for the onslaught, and within seconds, he felt the impact of the snow thudding into him. Over and over he rolled and eventually came to a halt. He began to take stock of his situation. There was clearly a huge amount of snow on top of him, but because it had not compacted down on him, he could wriggle around a little - though not enough to allow him to dig his way out; nor could he tell whether he was upside down or sideways on. He had lost his skis, but one of the ski-sticks was still attached to his wrist. There he was, miles away from anyone, under the snow. He knew that he could last for a certain amount of time because there was air within his little capsule, somewhat similar to being in a small igloo, but eventually, unless rescued, he would die of exposure. It was about seven in the morning.

Meanwhile, at home, when it got to about 9 o'clock, his Mother and Father became very concerned. He was long overdue. By the time they had contacted their friends and neighbours, it was 9.30, and it took them a further 30 minutes to reach the location Jacob would have made for. By 10 o'clock they had found him, thanks only to the fact that Jacob had gone to the village dance the previous night.

While Jacob had been taking stock of his situation buried under four feet of snow, he found in his pocket the bright red stub of the ticket from the dance. He managed to stick the ticket on to the point of the ski stick, and the ski stick through the snow to the open air above him. As soon as they arrived in the likely area, the rescue party scanned the vast expanse of snow. The only sight which caught the eye was the blood-red ticket.

If, then, you are likely to ski up the Alps to check your herd of chamois, then make sure that you go to a dance the night before and keep the stub of your red entrance ticket.

SURVIVING AND COPING AT SCHOOL: 1

SURVIVAL TECHNIQUES IN THE WILD

It is as likely that you will need the following information about as much as that you are likely to be raising chamois - but one never knows! The S.A.S. Survival Manual gives advice on these topics.

FOOD IN THE WILD

•INSECTS AND WORMS ...

Best served boiled. They should be cooked and then crushed in a can. A more acceptable method would be to dry them on hot rocks and then grind them into a powder which can then be used to enrich soups and stew.

•CROCODILES AND ALLIGATORS ...

The best meat comes from the tail, and is firm and very tasty.

MAKING A SHELTER   O.H.P. 2

1. Find any sort of a natural hollow then make a roof to keep the rain off and the warmth inside. Place a sturdy log across the top which in its turn can support lighter branches at a pitched angle. The roof can be consolidated with turf or twigs and the pitch will ensure that water drains off.

2. With a piece of plastic, canvas or a ground sheet it is possible to make very easily a number of effective shelters. One of the methods is illustrated below:

   (i) Make a triangular shelter with the apex pointing into the wind.

   (ii) Stake or weigh down the edges - if the material you have is long enough, then curl it underneath you.

   (iii) Cover the floor of the shelter with dry grass or bracken. Never lie on frozen, cold or damp ground.

SURVIVING AND COPING AT SCHOOL: 1

CONFRONTATIONS WITH DANGEROUS ANIMALS

The following appears to be excellent advice if you have nerves of steel, have worked with wild animals in a game-reserve for twenty years, or are simply mad!

O.H.P. 3

CONCLUSION

There may come a time in the future when some pupils will be under pressure to perform to the demands of the S.A.S. and survive in an environment where there is no ready shelter and they are required to live off the land. However, it is the day to day problems which the majority will have to resolve. Sometimes the chance to avoid a runaway rhinoceros might be a welcome diversion in a life which might seem to be fraught with less soluble difficulties.

SCRIPTURE READING
Ephesians, Chapter 6: verses 13-17

"Therefore, take up God's armour; then you will be able to stand your ground when things are at their worst, to complete every task and still to stand. Stand firm, I say. Buckle on the belt of truth; for coat of mail put on integrity; let the shoes on your feet be the Gospel of peace, to give you a firm footing; and, with all these, take up the great shield of faith, with which you will be able to quench all the flaming arrows of the evil one. Take salvation for helmet; for sword, take that which the spirit gives you - the words that come from God."

SURVIVING AND COPING AT SCHOOL: 1
MATERIAL FOR O.H.P.

O.H.P. 1

AN ALPINE SCENE

O.H.P. 2

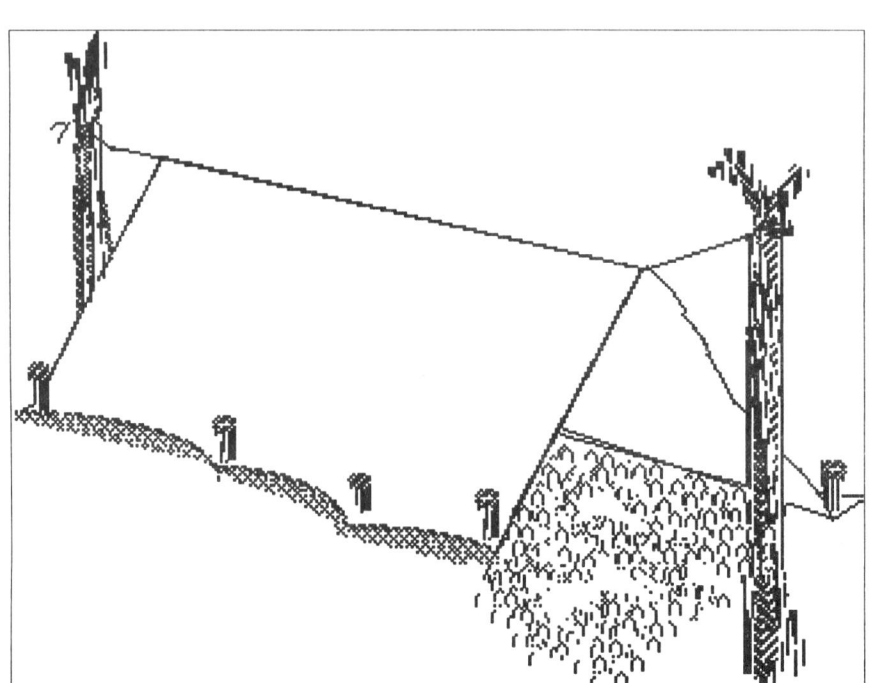

MAKING A SHELTER
(From The S.A.S. Survival Manual)

SURVIVING AND COPING AT SCHOOL: 1
MATERIAL FOR O.H.P. (Continued)

O.H.P. 3

CONFRONTATIONS WITH DANGEROUS ANIMALS

Attacks by animals are rare, but animals can be dangerous. Keep out of their way. If you confront one, it will be as surprised as you. Self-control will be needed, or you may unintentionally provoke the animal to attack.

- If you come face to face with a large animal - **FREEZE**. Slowly back off, and talk in a calm manner. In most cases the animal will back off too. Avoid making sudden movements, and remember that animals can smell fear - many a hunter has fouled his breeches and given himself away. Do your best to calm yourself.

- If an animal appears to charge, it may be that you are blocking its escape route. Move out of the way.

- If an animal seems determined to give chase (or you haven't got the nerve to freeze or side-step), zig-zag when you run - animals such as rhinos charge in a straight line and have poor eye-sight.

- A skilled nocturnal predator such as a leopard or tiger has excellent vision if you are on the move - though its colour vision is poor and it cannot see stationary objects well. Freeze if you have not already been sighted.

SURVIVING AND COPING AT SCHOOL: 1

SUGGESTED RESOURCES ...

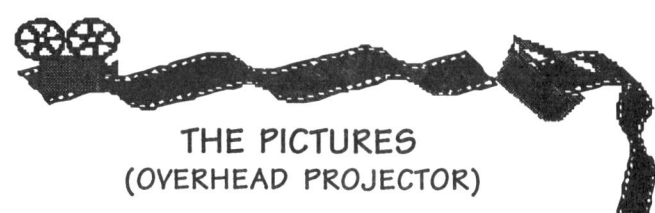

THE PICTURES
(OVERHEAD PROJECTOR)

- An Alpine Scene
- S.A.S. Survival Shelter
- Confrontations with Dangerous Animals

THE MUSIC

- "We Shall Overcome" - Joan Baez
- "You Ain't Seen Nothin' Yet" - Bachman-Turner Overdrive
- "Stayin' Alive" - Bee Gees
- "With A Little Help From My Friends" - Joe Cocker
- "You Can Get It If You Really Want" - Desmond Dekker
- "He Don't Hang Around With The Gang No More" - The Shangri-las
- "I Am A Rock" - Simon and Garfunkel
- "Write Me a Song" - Fivepenny Piece
- "Help!" - The Beatles

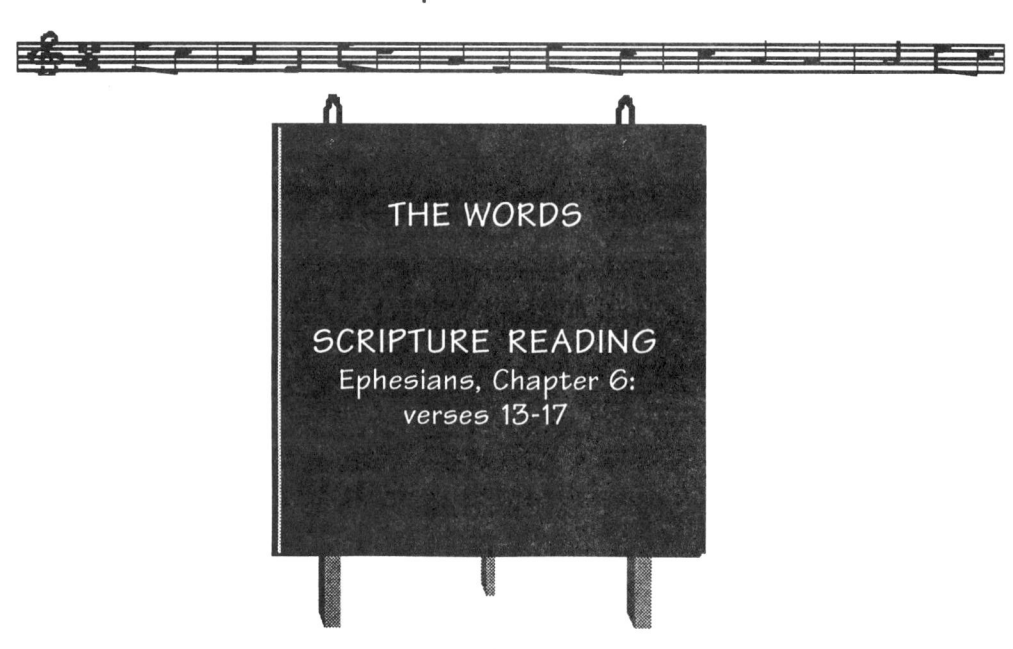

THE WORDS

SCRIPTURE READING
Ephesians, Chapter 6:
verses 13-17

SURVIVING AND COPING AT SCHOOL: 2

INTRODUCTION ...

Everyone at some time or another, regardless of occupation, wealth or position, is subject to particular tensions and anxieties. Pupils are no exception and, in order to begin to overcome and manage those stresses and strains, they need to be aware of what they are likely to be. Having identified them, then they can start to find strategies to cope with them. The main areas of pressure are:

O.H.P. 1

- PARENTS -
- SCHOOL WORK -
- STREET CREDIBILITY -
- CLOTHES -
- BULLIES -
- DRUGS -
- SEX -

PARENTS

Parents want what is best for their children, and quite naturally have every right and duty to encourage, cajole and urge as they think fit. It is not easy for caring parents to find the balance between firm coaxing and what sounds to children to be nagging or criticism. It is one of the prices offspring have to pay for having devoted and resolute guardians. The knowledge on the part of children that parents are trying to do what they consider is best may not reduce the haranguing but may explain it.

O.H.P. 2

SCHOOL WORK

The production of work of an acceptable quality is a fact of school life and part of the education process. It is a pressure which increases at examination times and varies according to Year Groups. However, the best way to cope with such pressure is to allocate and organise the required amount of time throughout the weeks and months. In other words - hard work and graft!

O.H.P. 3

SURVIVING AND COPING AT SCHOOL: 2

STREET CREDIBILITY and CLOTHES

Street credibility is the displaying of attitudes, behaviour and fashion which are appropriate and acceptable to an individual's peers or equals. To be identified and welcomed is important to young people, who intensely feel the need to gain approval and a sense of belonging.

It is difficult for youngsters to appreciate that there will come a time when "street cred." matters little and that the perceptions of their peers will diminish in significance the more independent and older they become.

This can be pointed out, but it is a difficult, and probably unrealistic, task to persuade them to be their own person.

O.H.P. 4

BULLIES

There are few of us who have not at one time or another had to put up with bullying. The individuals who inflict this torment are the abominations of youth. It is rarely the physical attacks which cause the pain, but rather the snide, callous, vicious and usually cowardly remarks and conspiracies which target perceived weaknesses.

In any establishment an anti-bullying culture has to be created through regular condemnation of this phenomenon, and a clear message regularly proclaimed which spells out firm sanctions.

It is an unfortunate aspect of school life that there will be bullies who, for whatever psychological hang-up, feel the need to oppress weaker members of the community. It is worth pointing out that the problem lies with the bully and not with the individual being bullied, but sadly that is small comfort while the victim is suffering what seems to them to be endless programme of agony and misery.

O.H.P. 5

DRUGS

O.H.P. 6

There seems little doubt that the problem of drugs is endemic within our society. Young people will at some time, if it has not transpired already, be put in the situation where they will be offered the opportunity or pressurised into experimenting. This applies, of course, to Nicotine, Marijuana and Alcohol but more specifically and sinisterly to drugs such as Ecstasy, Cocaine and Heroin.

It is said that "shock tactics" have little effect in moderating behaviour in this matter, but the words of the grieving parents of Leah Betts, who appeared on television in November 1995, on the day their daughter died in Broomfield Hospital, Chelmsford, five days after taking an Ecstasy tablet at her birthday party, may have some impact. Her mother said:

"I could lecture you like a mother until I am blue in the face, but the only people who can prevent this sort of thing happening again are yourselves. Remember that the drug that Leah took was pure. I am talking to you so that you can see the terrible effects of drugs on a beautiful young girl. To people who say that it was her own fault, then they are right. But Ecstasy killed my daughter, and drugs should not be available. If it is the fashion that drugs be taken, then it is a fashion which must die as our daughter has died."

A leading neurologist on the same day Leah died, 16 November 1995, said: "What the case of Leah has made very clear is that **Ecstasy kills** - the tablet she took was not part of a 'rogue batch' which contained adulterated chemicals. Small amounts of Ecstasy can kill and can affect the chemistry of the brain. Those who have taken the drug in the past can, additionally, be prone to depression and suicide."

SURVIVING AND COPING AT SCHOOL: 2

SEX

As with drugs, the climate of the society in which we live trivialises and cheapens sex. This puts intense pressure upon young people to experiment with, and become involved in, sexual activity before they are mature enough to handle it. That sexual relations should be the natural progression from a deep caring relationship, based on love and respect, is something which needs to be emphasised, and is a point of view which is applauded and welcomed by a surprising number of teenagers.

O.H.P. 7

CONCLUSION

The pressures, then, on young people are intense and in some cases very severe. It helps for them to be aware that the stresses and strains are not unique to them, and that everyone, to a greater or lesser degree, has had to face up to and resolve similar difficulties. If the troubles are only school-based - which they can be in a large number of instances - then it might be some consolation to mention that school life has only to be endured for what is, relatively speaking, a very short time. However, this is not always helpful when, in the perception of youth, a week can seem an eternity.

An emphasis upon, and encouragement of, confidence and independence - two attributes which can go a long way in handling and alleviating anxiety - might be promoted and encouraged.

Pupils need to understand that there are always friends, teachers and parents who are not only prepared to help in any way they can, but have a positive desire to do so.

SCRIPTURE READING:
I Corinthians, Chapter 9: verses 24-27

Surely you know that many runners take part in a race, but only one of them wins the prize. Run, then, in such a way as to win the prize. Every athlete in training submits to strict discipline, in order to be crowned with a wreath that will not last; but we do it for one that will last forever. That is why I run straight for the finishing line; that is why I am like a boxer who does not waste his punches. I harden my body with blows and bring it under complete control, to keep myself from being disqualified after having called others to the contest.

SURVIVING AND COPING AT SCHOOL: 2
MATERIAL FOR O.H.P.

O.H.P. 1

PRESSURES AT SCHOOL ...

- **PARENTS**
- **SCHOOL WORK**
- **STREET CREDIBILITY**
- **CLOTHES**
- **BULLIES**
- **DRUGS**
- **SEX**

O.H.P. 2

O.H.P. 3

SURVIVING AND COPING AT SCHOOL: 2
MATERIAL FOR O.H.P.
(Continued)

O.H.P. 4

O.H.P. 5

O.H.P. 6

O.H.P. 7

SURVIVING AND COPING AT SCHOOL: 2

SUGGESTED RESOURCES ...

THE PICTURES
(OVERHEAD PROJECTOR)

- Main Pressures on Young People (Summary)
- Parents
- School Work
- Street Credibility and • Clothes
- Bullies
- Drugs
- Sex

THE MUSIC

- "We Shall Overcome" - Joan Baez
- "You Ain't Seen Nothin' Yet" - Bachman-Turner Overdrive
- "Stayin' Alive" - Bee Gees
- "With A Little Help From My Friends" - Joe Cocker
- "You Can Get It If You Really Want" - Desmond Dekker
- "He Don't Hang Around With The Gang No More" - The Shangri-las
- "I Am A Rock" - Simon and Garfunkel
- "Write Me a Song" - Fivepenny Piece
- "Help!" - The Beatles
- "Under Pressure" - Queen

THE WORDS

SCRIPTURE READING:
I Corinthians, Chapter 9: verses 24-27

POTENTIAL

INTRODUCTION ...

So often we underestimate our own potential and can pass through life without really knowing what we could have achieved because we have not tried. Potential, from the Latin *"potens"* ("powerful"), means a capacity to achieve, and will never be exploited until we take up challenges. Too often the fear of failure deters us. Frightened that our image might be tarnished, our street-credibility dented, we take no chances. Failure has become a pejorative term, when it is a necessary prerequisite for maturity. To fail is to learn and develop; to become a more sensitive and understanding individual. While we should not *seek* failure, we should accept it and treat it as a regular part of life which helps us to progress to better things.

O.H.P. 1

In India the elephants which move the timber are tethered as babies by a rope attached to a stake in the ground. They cannot move beyond the length of the rope because they are firmly tethered and do not have the strength to pull the stake out. When they do get bigger, stronger and heavier, they could yank the stake out with ease, but because they still believe, as they did when smaller, that they cannot escape, they do not make the effort. They have the potential, but do not use it because, psychologically, they believe they cannot. Very often we do not appreciate our potential because it is never tested.

O.H.P. 2

POTENTIAL

Sometimes we realise our potential because we find ourselves in situations where we have to cope in order to survive.

STORY

This is well demonstrated by the story of Jules and Susanne Defré during the last War. Jules, a prominent member of the French Underground in Lyons, was tipped off that he was due to be arrested. He headed for Nîmes, Foix, and beyond to the Pyrenees, to cross into neutral Spain with young wife, Susanne, their daughter, Claudette, and Susanne's older sister, Nicole, who, an orphan like Susanne, always lived with the family. At Foix, they bought emergency rations, sleeping bags and medical supplies for the journey, and made for the foot-hills of the Pyrenees and the high Pico de Aneto. It was February, and soon they left the cedar, pine and oak forests and trudged on and on, forever upwards. Susanne took the lead, followed by her sister, carrying the haversack of supplies. Jules brought up the rear, carrying 18-month-old Claudette. In the distance, Susanne could see the white-capped mountains, and dreaded the climb. Since childhood her phobia had been heights, and from the age of 13 had been unable to climb spiralling staircases, or any stairway which gave any view of a drop. As she led the way onto the barely visible track at the base of the mountain, fear gripped her stomach and a giddiness filled her head. She knew she had no choice - by now the Nazis would be seeking them, and would be looking to the Pyrenees more closely than ever.

Gradually the path grew steeper and became narrower. Ice, covered by a thin layer of powdery snow, lay on the path; each step brought her nearer to the edge of the mountain, but, head down, she carefully watched each step her feet made. Higher and higher they made their way, and now she could sense, rather than see, that a huge chasm was now located on her right hand side. Her clothes were damp, and she knew it was the dampness of fear mingling with the perspiration of effort. She trembled as she moved forward - then suddenly she slipped as she made to turn a corner on the narrow pathway. She fell forward onto her outstretched hands, with her head and shoulders hanging over the void. Hundreds of feet below, the huge trees which they had passed hours earlier appeared diminutive in the distance. She froze in a horror which only faded when she realised that, as she had fallen, her legs had pushed backwards and unbalanced her sister, Nicole, who was now sliding backwards towards the edge. Susanne got to her feet and lunged towards her sister, trying to grab the rucksack which was hampering her attempts to stop. Screaming with fear, she reached the edge, stopped, then with a piercing scream toppled over into the void. The biting wind choked the hysterical lament that came from the mouth of Susanne. She stared in disbelief at the spot where her sister had been moments earlier. Jules handed the child to his wife, and peered over the edge, expecting to see the body of Nicole hundreds of feet below - in fact, what he did see was his sister-in-law lying on a narrow ledge six feet below the path, her legs partly hanging over the chasm. Nicole was conscious, but clearly in great pain with a broken arm when he squeezed his feet one behind the other near her on the ledge. He took the rope from the haversack, threw it to Susanne, who tied it on to a jutting rock, and very slowly, Nicole was helped back onto the narrow path. Pain-killers from the medical supplies were given to her. Continued movement was essential for survival, and despite the desire of all three to just lie down and rest, they dragged themselves onwards in the realisation that to halt was to die. Within an hour, they had reached the pass, and were making their way to the Spanish town of Pobla de Segur and began to descend into Spain. As they forced themselves onwards, the temperature rose, the sun shone, and they knew they would be all right.

Susanne had overcome her fear of heights, Nicole her pain, and Jules with Claudette his weariness.

POTENTIAL

CONCLUSION

In the story, Susanne, petrified of heights, managed to conquer her fears when the need arose. Had she not found herself in that situation, then she would never have dreamed of attempting to scale the side of the mountain. Like Susanne, we all have hidden potential which, when we are called upon to demonstrate it in extreme circumstances, we are able to do so. However, that capacity is there, and we must have the confidence to challenge ourselves and to embrace every opportunity to test ourselves. Great fulfilment can be achieved by stretching our talents to the limits.

SCRIPTURE READING

Philippians, Chapter 3: verses 12-14

I do not claim that I have already succeeded or have already become perfect. I keep striving to win the prize for which Christ Jesus has already won me to Himself. Of course, my brothers, I really do not think that I have already won it; the one thing I do, however, is to forget what is behind me and do my best to reach what is ahead. So I run straight towards the goal in order to win the prize, which is God's call through Christ Jesus to the Life Above.

POTENTIAL
MATERIAL FOR O.H.P.

O.H.P. 1

O.H.P. 2

POTENTIAL

SUGGESTED RESOURCES ...

THE PICTURES
(OVERHEAD PROJECTOR)

- Two Elephants tied to a Stake
- Mountainous Region with Route marked in

THE MUSIC

- "Simply The Best" - Tina Turner
- "You Can Get It If You Really Want" - Desmond Dekker
- "I Wanna Be A Winner" - Brown Sauce
- "When The Going Gets Tough, The Tough Get Going" - Billy Ocean
- "I Can See Clearly Now" - Johnny Nash
- "No Frontiers" - Mary Black

THE WORDS

SCRIPTURE READING:

Philippians, Chapter 3:
verses 12-14

REMEMBRANCE DAY

INTRODUCTION ...

75 years ago, on the 11th day of the 11th month at the 11th hour, the First World War came to an end. Next Sunday is **REMEMBRANCE SUNDAY**, the special day set aside each year when we remember all of those this Century who have died in the Wars from the First World War onwards.

In the days before-hand, many people wear a poppy - which is the **FLOWER OF REMEMBRANCE**. This custom of wearing poppies derives from a poem which was written in 1915, during the War, by a man called **John McCrae**, a medical officer with the Canadian Army. He wrote the poem when there was a lull in the fighting when he was in charge of a small first-aid station at Ypres. He himself died in 1918 after being wounded.

IN FLANDERS' FIELDS

O.H.P. 1

The money raised by selling poppies goes to help those who have been disabled through war, and the families of those who have been killed.

MANY WERE KILLED

If you look at the numbers of fatalities in the Wars in which Britain has been involved in this Century alone, you will see that there have been very many who have been killed.

O.H.P. 2

THE FIRST WORLD WAR

If any of you ever travel to France, to Paris or to Spain, by coach or by car, you are almost certain to drive over the very ground where the battles of the First World War were fought, and where so many thousands of men were killed. Now, of course, it is peaceful and clean with beautiful trees, little farm-houses and neat fields where once there was only mud and barbed wire.

Some of you may have visited one of the very many War Memorials which have been built in honour of those who died, or one of the hundreds of cemeteries where they have been buried.

REMEMBRANCE DAY

O.H.P. 3

VIMY RIDGE

One of the most impressive is the memorial at **VIMY RIDGE**. The Memorial is built on the ridge which was held by the Germans and was of vital importance to them because it protected factories and mines, and as well as the defence systems running north to the coast.

At a cost of 3,000 dead and 10,600 wounded, the ridge was taken on 9/10 April 1916. The Memorial was raised to the 60,000 Canadians who died in World War I, and inscribed on the ramparts of the Memorial are the names of 11,285 Canadian soldiers who were posted as "MISSING, PRESUMED DEAD" in France.

THE BATTLE OF VIMY RIDGE

On 9 June 1917 the day dawned bright and warm. The shells which had been pounding the enemy positions on the ridge at Vimy for the whole of the previous week had just stopped. The only sound there was in the warm morning air was that of the few birds which had entered the skies above the battle area. George Kerr, a 20-year-old lieutenant in the Canadian Army, was waiting for the signal to advance across No-Man's Land with his squad of ten men to attack the German trenches which were less than 100 yards away.

The signal was due at 7.00 a.m. At 6.55 there was a deep silence, even though within a small area there were as many as 100,000 soldiers ready to give battle. In each man's thoughts was the possibility that this could well be his last day on this Earth. Each was lost in his own private thoughts.

Suddenly the whistle sounded - the chilling sound that meant the time for attack had arrived and, with shouts and screams, 30,000 Canadians yelled their war-cries as they jumped from their trenches and ran, bent double, towards the enemy lines. George led his men over the top of the trench and, with his second-in-command, Corporal Bill Harding, sprinted with the other nine men towards the enemy position.

The sound of rifle and machine gun fire crackled all around, and George could see in front of him men suddenly pulling up short as they felt the impact of the bullet hitting them. Bullets and explosions grew heavier the further he went, and as he stumbled across the land which had been torn apart by the bombs and shells, he thought he heard a shout from Bill Harding. It was quickly forgotten as he struggled onwards and fought for his own survival.

Eventually he reached the enemy trench, forced his way in, and the life or death struggle with the enemy began. Ten minutes' bitter fighting with pistol and bayonet resulted in George's squad clearing the area of enemy trench they had been designated. It was only then that he was able to take stock of the situation and see

REMEMBRANCE DAY

THE BATTLE OF VIMY RIDGE
(Continued)

who was left. Out of the 10 men there were only 5 remaining, and amongst them there was no sign of Bill Harding. George remembered the shout that he had heard, and looked back over the land across which he had only just come.

There amongst the fallen soldiers he saw an arm held high in the air, as if in a plea for help. He recognised, about 40 yards away, the figure and the face of Bill. The battle was now at its height, with bullets cascading down upon No-Man's Land from both directions, but without any regard for his own safety, George immediately left the protection of the trench, and made his way, on hands and knees, towards his Corporal and his friend.

When eventually he reached Bill, he found that a bullet had shattered the bone in his right leg, and another had gone through the fleshy part of his shoulder. George realised that, if he could get Bill back to the safety of the trench, then he could be saved. He half-carried, half-dragged Bill towards the rest of his men who, above the gun-fire, screamed encouragement. George finally reached the trench, jumped in, and his men gently began to pull Bill in after him. Just as they were dragging him over the parapet, a bullet hit Bill in the temple. He died instantly.

The saddest thing of all was that the bullet had come from a Canadian soldier who, in his panic, thought that Bill was a German soldier re-entering a German trench.

George, as the officer in charge of Bill, collected his possessions together to send them to his family. There wasn't much - a wallet with a few letters from his wife, and a well-used photograph of himself, his wife, and his two lads, aged 5 and 7.

George received the Victoria Cross for bravery. Bill was buried at Vimy Ridge, and you can go and see his name engraved on the ramparts of the Memorial.

CONCLUSION

Whatever the reasons for war, and whether you think there are times when wars are inevitable and should happen, there is no doubt that they bring with them pain and agony, death and destruction. They leave kids without fathers, and women without husbands. For those involved, the only thing you can be sure they do bring is misery.

REMEMBRANCE DAY

SCRIPTURE READING
St. John, Chapter 14: verses 1-6

"Set your troubled hearts at rest. Trust in God always; trust also in Me. There are many dwelling-places in my Father's house; if it were not so, I should have told you; for I am going there on purpose to prepare a place for you. And if I go and prepare a place for you, I shall come again and receive you to Myself, so that where I am you may be also; and my way there is known to you." Thomas said: "Lord - We do not know where You are going, so how can we know the way?" Jesus replied: "I am the way; I am the truth, and I am life; no-one comes to the Father except by Me ..."

REMEMBRANCE DAY
MATERIAL FOR O.H.P.

O.H.P. 1

IN FLANDERS' FIELDS

In Flanders' fields the poppies blow
Between the crosses, row on row
    That mark our place; and in the sky
    The larks, still bravely singing, fly
Scarce heard amid the guns below.

We are the Dead. Short days ago
We lived, felt dawn, saw sunset glow,
    Loved and were loved, and now we lie
    In Flanders' fields.

Take up our quarrel with the foe:
To you from failing hands we throw
    The torch; be yours to hold it high.
    If ye break faith with us who die
We shall not sleep, though poppies grow
    In Flanders' fields.

O.H.P. 2

War Dead *(estimated)* : 20th Century

TOTAL DEATHS - MILITARY & CIVILIAN

World War I (1914-1918)	8,600,000
World War II (1939-1945)	22,709,937
Korean War (1950-1953)	3,459,360
Falklands War (1982)	984
Gulf War	343
	(civilians unknown)
Northern Ireland	3,100

TOTAL : 34,773,724

REMEMBRANCE DAY

SUGGESTED RESOURCES ...

THE PICTURES
(OVERHEAD PROJECTOR)

- "In Flanders' Fields"
- War Dead Statistics
- Vimy Ridge

THE MUSIC

- "Peace Will Come" - Tom Paxton
- "Universal Soldier" - Donovan
- "Born In The U.S.A." - Bruce Springsteen
- "Peace Train" - Cat Stevens
- "The Green Fields Of France" - The Fureys
- "Imagine" - John Lennon
- "Give Peace A Chance" - John Lennon
- "I Don't Want To Be A Soldier" - John Lennon
- "Farewell, Angelina" - Joan Baez
- "Soldier" - Harvey Andrews
- "19" - Paul Hardcastle

THE WORDS

SCRIPTURE READING
St. John, Chapter 14: verses 1-6

PASSING TESTS: 1

INTRODUCTION ...

Whether we like it or not we live in a competitive and demanding World where, if we wish to succeed in terms of gaining meaningful employment, we need to pass tests and be selected. The first check that employers make on any applicant is the school record. They are interested in what academic qualifications have been gained, and whether such qualities as co-operation, honesty, loyalty and an ability to get on with others are prominent characteristics. Depending upon the nature and the needs of the career to which we may aspire, there will be other skills which are required.

SELECTION FOR THE S.A.S.

The S.A.S. (Special Air Services) is renowned throughout the World as a unit within the British Forces for its professionalism, efficiency and outstanding qualities of performance and courage. It only selects from the very best of those who apply from the three Services, the Army, Navy and Royal Air Force. Less than ten per cent of applicants are selected after the most rigorous and demanding tests of any fighting force in the World. These tests are designed to assess whether an individual has the necessary physical, intellectual and temperamental make-up to carry out the arduous and formidable operations required of this elite unit over the World. Marches through the desolate regions of the Brecon Beacons are standard, but an analysis of psychological disposition is measured by a series of one-off situations in which the volunteers are placed. Here are two of them.

BLUE RIBBON PERFORMANCE!

PASSING TESTS: 1

THE TRAIN `O.H.P. 1`

Would-be recruits are blindfolded and led outside, where they are laid across a railway-track and attached to one of the lines by a handcuff and a length of chain. In the distance they can hear a steam train approaching their location. Those who keep cool and show their initiative realise that they have enough slack in the chain to roll over beside the line to which the chain has been attached. Those who panic, as the train advances nearer and nearer, begin to shout out, and with their free hand rip off the blindfold. They will then see that there are two parallel rail-tracks close together, and that they have been laid across those which the approaching train is not using.

THE LONG DISTANCE 'YOMP' `O.H.P. 2`

Would-be recruits are taken on a 40 mile route-march with full pack which they have to complete in a fixed time. As they near the end of the march, they can see the trucks parked which are there to take them back to barracks, a hot bath and food. When they are within a couple of hundred metres of the lorries, they start up and move away. The soldiers are then told by the Instructors that they have to continue marching for another ten miles. It is at this stage that the faint-hearted drop out, while those who continue are relieved to find the trucks out of sight around the next corner.

BLUE RIBBON PERFORMANCE!

PASSING TESTS: 1

CONCLUSION

Above have been described only two of the tests designed to test the mettle of those who aspire to the S.A.S.. Others are equally taxing, such as having to scale cliffs during training, with live ammunition being used by the instructors aimed at just missing those climbing; or having to jump a gap of three metres from a cliff to a narrow, isolated pinnacle of rock, four metres in diameter, with a drop of 95 metres.

It is highly unlikely that many of us will ever be subject to such severe, even brutal, procedures, when seeking a chosen career, but there is no escaping the fact that preference in the world of work will be awarded to those who have earned it through effort and achievement. Rare indeed is the individual who obtains his or her desired occupation in life by someone coming along and offering it to them without struggle of some sort. Logically, then, it would seem to be worth the endeavour to make the best possible use of the opportunities and chances offered at school.

PRAYER

Lord, Give us the strength and perseverance to make the most of our life at School; to use our time wisely and constructively, so that the talents which we all have can be developed and increased. Help to build up within us the confidence to tackle the tasks we are given to the best of our abilities, so that we can look back on the period we have spent here, and can say we have made the most of our opportunities.

BLUE RIBBON PERFORMANCE!

PASSING TESTS: 1

SUGGESTED RESOURCES ...

THE PICTURES
(OVERHEAD PROJECTOR)

- Examples of S.A.S. Exercises

THE MUSIC

- "Under Pressure" - Queen
- "One Moment In Time" - Whitney Houston
* "I Want It All" - Queen

THE WORDS

A PRAYER
(Sheet 7.3)

BLUE RIBBON PERFORMANCE!

PASSING TESTS: 2

INTRODUCTION ...

Examinations and tests of one sort or another are now a compulsory and intrinsic aspect of school life from an early age. Academic achievement with their levels of attainment figure largely and intellectual potential is tested when other talents are diminished. The girl who is accomplished at judo, and the boy who is proficient in kite-making, need to be encouraged and applauded. Each of us has skills and talents which will never impact upon the National Curriculum, but which should be a source of pride, confidence and self-esteem.

However, it remains a fact of life that pupils are called upon to take tests, and as such must strive to maximise their talents. It is also a fact that individuals have a tendency to sell themselves short and under-estimate their own abilities. The excuse "I'm not good enough" is frequently not a comment upon one's aptitude, but on self-confidence and application. A French saying sums up this self-deprecation: ***"Nature has concealed at the bottom of our minds talents and abilities of which we are not aware."***

We only have to look around to see individuals who, with disabilities we shall never know, have attained breath-taking levels of performance in numerous spheres of activity.

As in many cases of success, the significant ingredients have been the preparation and effort made. Guidelines have been drawn up, under various headings, which might be of assistance in helping pupils to make the most of their talents as they progress through the demands of the National Curriculum.   `O.H.P. 1` to `O.H.P. 7`

- Be Disciplined
- Using Your Time Efficiently
- Keep Fit!
- Get Help Early and Start Preparing Early
- Enhancing Your Concentration
- Improving Your Memory
- Preparing Just Before the Examination - The Final Few Weeks

PRAYER ...   `O.H.P. 8`

PASSING TESTS: 2
MATERIAL FOR O.H.P.

Be Disciplined ... — O.H.P. 1

- **Draw up a timetable of study tasks – plan your revision and stipulate exactly what you intend to do in each hour or half-hour. Keep to it.**

- **Break up large revision jobs into more manageable tasks.**

- **Establish deadlines for revision of each subject.**

- **Use rewards to reinforce progress**

Using Your Time Efficiently ... — O.H.P. 2

Assess critically your time commitments to the following:

- Television
- Idle waiting time
- Unnecessarily long telephone calls
- Drop-in visitors
- Time wasted because you could not say "No!"

If you really want to do something, build it into your Revision Timetable and **KEEP TO IT**.

Keep Fit! ... — O.H.P. 3

- Eat a well-balanced diet
- Do not worry about the loss of a few hours of sleep before the exams
- Maintain a regular exercise programme
- Anticipate any problems which might arise and resolve them beforehand - it helps to avoid panic and promote confidence.

GET HELP EARLY AND START PREPARING EARLY ... — O.H.P. 4

- SEEK HELP FROM: TEACHING STAFF AND CLASSMATES
- KNOW THE SYLLABUS AND WHAT WILL BE EXAMINED
- KNOW THE EXAM FORMAT - YOU MUST **LOOK AT PAST PAPERS**
- KNOW EXACTLY WHAT EQUIPMENT YOU WILL NEED FOR EACH EXAMINATION
- HAVE A CLEAR TIMETABLE OF <u>WHEN</u> AND <u>WHERE</u> THE EXAMINATION WILL BE HELD
- MAKE MAXIMUM USE OF **REVISION LESSONS**

PASSING TESTS: 2
MATERIAL FOR O.H.P.
(Continued)

O.H.P. 5

Enhancing Your Concentration ...

- Establish firm and fixed times, and set places for studying
- Get rid of distractions
- Make sure your place of study is ...

  Quiet
  Comfortable
  Well lit
  Well ventilated
  Distraction-free

- **Be positive** - it is always difficult to revise tasks that do not interest you, but they have to be faced

O.H.P. 6

Improving Your Memory ...

- Revise early
- Read through your notes five or more times
- Recite the material you are learning
- Write very brief notes to ensure you do know the material
- Repeat the above as frequently as possible
- Learn difficult lists by using mnemonics
- Carry Revision Cards and Check-lists with you
- Use drawings, bubbles, etc., to aid visual recall

O.H.P. 7 — PREPARING JUST BEFORE THE EXAMINATION - THE FINAL FEW WEEKS

- Construct weekly, daily, even hourly study session plans
- Account for differences in subject complexity and personal interest when planning your revision schedules
- Make sure every study goal is task- and time-specific
- Allocate your time in proportion to the importance of the subject areas and the marks available
- Cram only as a last resort - Spaced, regular learning is far preferable
- Plan to take study breaks to rest your mind, but be disciplined about time

O.H.P. 8 — PRAYER

Lord, Help us in our examinations and tests. For everyone who has to take them, they cause stress and concern and, as such, they are something we would all rather do without. However, since they are a necessary part of our existence, support and comfort us in our efforts, and help us to have the confidence to make the most of our chances. We in our turn appreciate that we can expect nothing without hard work and study.

PASSING TESTS: 2

SUGGESTED RESOURCES ...

THE PICTURES
(OVERHEAD PROJECTOR)

• Strategies and Techniques for an Effective Revision Programme

THE MUSIC

• "Under Pressure" - Queen
• "One Moment In Time" - Whitney Houston
• "I Want It All" - Queen

THE WORDS

A PRAYER
(Sheet 8.3)

CAUSES OF TROUBLE AT HOME

INTRODUCTION ...

Mark Twain once said: *"When I was a boy of fourteen, my father was so ignorant I could hardly stand to have the old man around. But when I got to twenty-one, I was astonished at how much he had learned in seven years."*

It is an inevitable fact of life that as children are progressing through adolescence and establishing their own values and independence they will come into conflict with their parents, who have the unenviable duty of trying to advise and control their offspring. The degree of control varies, of course, depending upon the good sense of both parties, but as a general rule the sources of disharmony are much of a muchness.

The following causes of **domestic discord** between parents and children are not in rank order ...

`O.H.P. 1`

- TIME TO BE IN AT NIGHT
- UNTIDINESS/CLEANING UP
- BROTHERS/SISTERS
- APPEARANCE/CLOTHES
- MONEY
- GETTING UP IN THE MORNING
- HOMEWORK
- CHOICE OF FRIENDS
- THE TELEPHONE
- LOUD MUSIC
- BATHROOM/HAIR DRYER

PARENTAL ATTITUDES `O.H.P. 2`

It is not difficult for even the most anti-authoritarian daughter or son to understand, even if they disagree, why it is in this day and age, that parents insist on certain restrictions, guidelines and rules for their children. Whether we like it or not, there are potential threats and dangers existing within our society from which any caring parents would seek to guard their offspring. The incidence of drug-taking, assault, thieving, sex attacks, drunkenness and mindless violence put an enormous responsibility and strain upon mothers and fathers who are trying to protect and do what is best for the children they love. It is difficult for parents to achieve the right balance - not to be too inflexible and at the same time to permit the latitude required for development and peace at home. The acid test for a discontented child is to ask herself or himself the measure of freedom which s/he would give her/his children if s/he had any in the future - and to answer *honestly*.

Furthermore, it is only right and proper that, within the family community, there should be a reasonableness with **everyone** pulling their weight, working at creating and maintaining peace in the home, and not abusing the facilities and the generosity of parents. Again it is reasonable for children to consider how they would expect anyone to behave and treat the house if it belonged to them.

CAUSES OF TROUBLE AT HOME

POINTERS TO PEACE AT HOME ...

- REALISE THAT YOUR PARENTS ARE TRYING TO DO WHAT IS BEST FOR YOU
- ALWAYS BE REASONABLE
- TRY AND SEE THEIR POINT OF VIEW
- KEEP CALM - NO TANTRUMS OR "FREAKING OUT"
- TALK ABOUT AND SHARE PROBLEMS
- BE READY TO COMPROMISE

CONCLUSION

It is the obligation of all members of the family to ensure that tranquillity reigns at home. All too often within a household there is something akin to a volcanic eruption over some trivial matter which at any other time would pale into insignificance in relation to other issues.

"The man who breaks his leg forgets the cold in his nose."

In addition, the old maxim still holds good: *"Jaw, jaw is better than war, war."*

SCRIPTURE READING:
Ephesians, Chapter 6: verses 2-4

"Children ... respect your Father and Mother" is the first Commandment that has a promise added: "... so that all may go well with you, and you may live a long time in the land."

Parents - do not treat your children in such a way as to make them angry. Instead, bring them up with Christian discipline and instruction.

CAUSES OF TROUBLE AT HOME

MATERIAL FOR O.H.P.

O.H.P. 1

- TIME TO BE IN AT NIGHT
- UNTIDINESS/CLEANING UP
- BROTHERS/SISTERS
- APPEARANCE/CLOTHES
- MONEY
- GETTING UP IN THE MORNING
- HOMEWORK
- CHOICE OF FRIENDS
- THE TELEPHONE
- LOUD MUSIC
- BATHROOM/HAIR DRYER

O.H.P. 2

POINTERS TO PEACE AT HOME ...

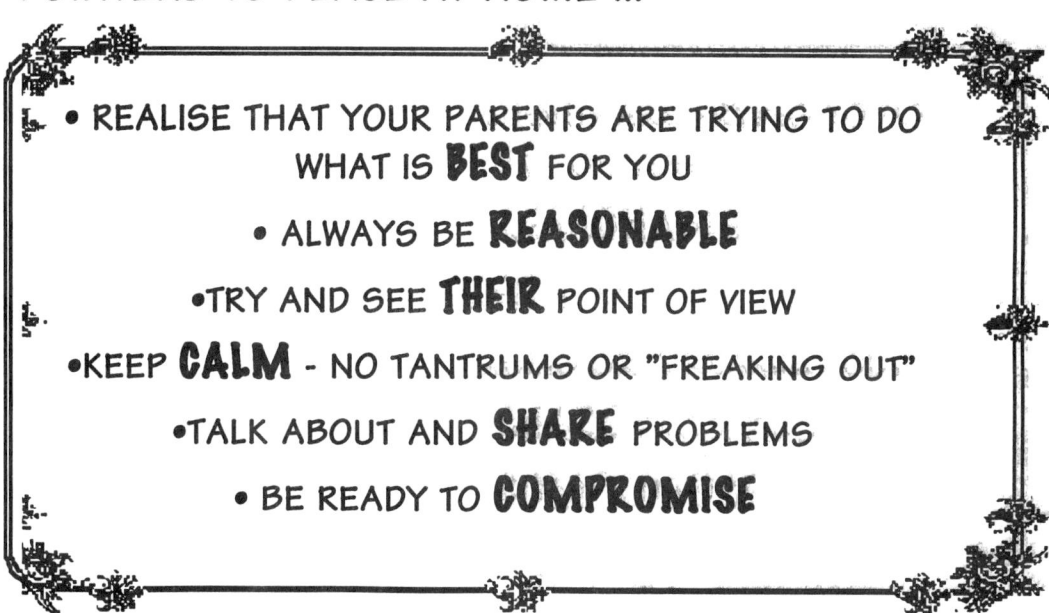

- REALISE THAT YOUR PARENTS ARE TRYING TO DO WHAT IS **BEST** FOR YOU
- ALWAYS BE **REASONABLE**
- TRY AND SEE **THEIR** POINT OF VIEW
- KEEP **CALM** - NO TANTRUMS OR "FREAKING OUT"
- TALK ABOUT AND **SHARE** PROBLEMS
- BE READY TO **COMPROMISE**

CAUSES OF TROUBLE AT HOME

MATERIAL FOR O.H.P.
(Continued)

O.H.P. 3

If only I had stayed
Anguish of the friend who left club early as lost Louise danced on

Store knife horror
Ten wounded as maniac goes on stabbing spree

Mother tells of family's grief after latest Ecstasy death

'Don't dance with death'
THIS is the message from the girl who almost lost her life taking the drug Ecstasy

Driver finds naked body of Celine dumped in a lay-by

Ten thousand volunteers fail to find missing girl

CAUSES OF TROUBLE AT HOME

SUGGESTED RESOURCES ...

THE PICTURES
(OVERHEAD PROJECTOR)

- Causes of Trouble at Home
- Pointers to Peace at Home
- Newspaper headlines highlighting dangers for young people on streets, e.g. accidents, drugs, ...

THE MUSIC

- "She's Leaving Home" - The Beatles
- "Going Back Home" - Boney M
- "Father and Son" - Cat Stevens/Boyzone
- "Peace Will Come" - Tom Paxton
- "Shades of Grey" - The Monkees
- "We Can Work It Out" - The Beatles
- "Matchstick Men and Matchstalk Cats and Dogs" - Brian and Michael
- "Warpaint" - Brook Brothers
- "If I Had A Hammer" - Trini Lopez
- "Our House" - Divine Madness
- "Without Love You Are Nothing" - Larry Norman

THE WORDS

SCRIPTURE READING
Ephesians, Chapter 6:
verses 2-4

IS THE GRASS REALLY GREENER ... ?

INTRODUCTION ...

Very frequently we become disenchanted with our lives and dissatisfied with our lot in life. What we take for granted, other people would long for, and we have a tendency to envy the life-style of others. We might covet their possessions, their wealth, their weather or their jobs, but if we were to change places with them, there is a fair chance that we would regret our new-found circumstances.

THE COLDEST PLACE IN THE WORLD

A man called Raoul de Gerona, who was a goldsmith by trade, lived in the South of Spain near Malaga. He loved the months of December, January and February on the Costa del Sol, but he dreaded the heat of the rest of the year, and particularly the months of May, June, July, August and September, when he found the heat, throughout the day and the night, very oppressive and uncomfortable. He liked to be outside in the open air, but found that during those months he had to seek shade under the trees or inside the house behind thick walls.

One day, while Raoul was reading a magazine on "Gold", he found amongst the adverts a job, for one year, in a town called Ustnera in Siberia in Russia. This town was the coldest inhabited place in the World, and though it had started out as a place where reindeer herders had gone, it had later become a centre for the manufacture of small, delicate gold items. This was because the inhabitants could do nothing else there in order to make money, but they could sit at home and make very ornate gold ornaments and trinkets out of transportable lumps of gold. It was like the Swiss who lived in their mountains and could not have any heavy industry or manufacturing up there so they concentrated on the production of watches and cuckoo-clocks, banking and yodelling.

Raoul decided that he would apply for the job and enjoy a year away from the heat of the sun and the incessant buzzing of the mosquitoes as they dive-bombed against his bare flesh at night. He had never seen snow nor made a snowball, and thought it would be a wonderful experience. He obtained the post for the year, kept his own job open, and off he went. He flew from Malaga to Moscow and caught a small plane to the town of Sutja and from there pursued the hundred mile journey to Utavet. When he got out of the plane at Sutja, he was completely unprepared for the intensity of the cold, but rapidly became acclimatised once he got into the car which was to take him to his final destination. As he travelled along, Raoul began to take in his surroundings. It was a bleak landscape as they travelled slowly on the ice-packed road. From the time they left the airport and the few houses around it until they arrived at Ustnera, where he was to work, he saw no sign of life or habitation. He noticed that the windows of the car were very thick indeed, and that the driver - who spoke no Spanish - looked not unlike Michelin man, with all the layers of woolly clothes he was wearing. An English-speaking work-mate quickly told him everything he needed to know ...

O.H.P. 1 MAP SHOWING LOCATION OF SIBERIA

IS THE GRASS REALLY GREENER ... ?

O.H.P. 2
CONDITIONS IN USTNERA

Very soon Raoul found himself dreaming of his home in Malaga, the sun, and even the mosquitoes. Never again would he curse the heat of summer!

O.H.P. 3

CONCLUSION

Let us be satisfied with what we have in life, make the best of it, and thank God for it!

SCRIPTURE READING
St. Mark, Chapter 12: verses 1-8
(The Parable of the Tenants in the Vineyard)

The story of men who, dissatisfied with what they had, wanted everything - with dire consequences.

Then Jesus spoke to them in parables:

"Once there was a man who planted a vineyard, put a fence round it, dug a hole for the wine-press, and built a watch-tower. Then he let out the vineyard to tenants and left home on a journey. When the time came to gather the grapes, he sent a servant to the tenants to receive from them his share of the harvest. The tenants seized the servant, beat him, and sent him back without a thing. Then the owner sent another servant: the tenants beat him over the head and treated him shamefully. The owner sent another servant, and they killed him; and they treated many others the same way, beating some and killing others. The only one left to send was the man's own dear son. Last of all, then, he sent his son to the tenants. 'I am sure they will respect my son,' he said. But those tenants said to one another: 'This is the owner's son. Come on - let's kill him, and his property will be ours!' So they seized the son and killed him, and threw his body out of the vineyard.

"What, then, will the owner of the vineyard do?" asked Jesus. "He will come and kill those men and hand the vineyard over to other tenants."

IS THE GRASS REALLY GREENER ... ?

ADDITIONAL MATERIAL ...

QUOTATIONS

- Blessed is he who has found his work; let him ask no other blessedness. *(Thomas Carlyle)*

- I want to be what I was when I wanted to be what I am now. *(Graffiti)*

HUMOUR

Richard Nixon met Ted Sorenson shortly after JFK's inaugural address, and remarked that there were things in the speech that he would have like to have said. Sorenson asked him whether it was the part about 'Ask not what your country can do for you ...' "No," replied Nixon. "- The part beginning: 'I do solemnly swear ...'"

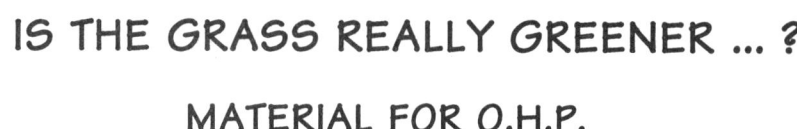

IS THE GRASS REALLY GREENER ... ?
MATERIAL FOR O.H.P.

O.H.P. 1

IS THE GRASS REALLY GREENER ... ?

MATERIAL FOR O.H.P.
(Continued)

O.H.P. 2

CONDITIONS IN USTNERA

- Winter temperatures hover between -60°C and -70°C
- Cars needed double glazing
- You could not stay outside in the cold for more than 4 hours at a time
- Goose fat had to be rubbed on to skin to protect it from peeling away and dropping off with the cold
- You must breathe through a scarf or your lungs would freeze up
- Contact lenses would freeze to your eye-balls
- You must keep your mouth closed, or your fillings would pop out
- Boots and coats made from man-made fibres would crack and fall apart
- Buttons would "pop off", if sewn on with synthetic thread
- You should wear mittens rather than gloves, or your fingers would freeze together
- The tiny hairs in your nose freeze instantly
- Milk comes in slabs
- A car would fall apart if it were hit with a hammer
- Pipes have to be at waist height because the ground is permanently frozen
- Every house has at least four doors and porches
- In Summer, a plague of mosquitoes descends

IS THE GRASS REALLY GREENER ... ?
MATERIAL FOR O.H.P.
(Continued)

O.H.P. 3

IS THE GRASS REALLY GREENER ... ?

SUGGESTED RESOURCES ...

THE PICTURES
(OVERHEAD PROJECTOR)

- Map showing where Siberia is
- Conditions in Ustnera
- OHPs of very hot and very cold places

THE MUSIC

- "That's The Way To Do It" - Dire Straits
- "I Want It All, And I Want It Now" - Queen
- "If I Were A Rich Man" - Roger Whittaker
- "O Lucky Man" - Alan Price
- "There But For Fortune" - Joan Baez
- "The Other Man's Grass" - Petula Clark
- "Mr. Businessman" - Ray Stevens
- "Born With A Smile On My Face" - Stephanie de Sykes
- "My Old Man's A Dustman" - Lonnie Donegan

THE WORDS

SCRIPTURE READING

St. Mark, Chapter 12: verses 1-8
The Parable of the Tenants in the Vineyard

THE BEST INTERPRETATION

INTRODUCTION ...

In a Christian Country such as our own, all Schools are based on the Gospel values, and one of the most crucial of these is to make every effort to put the best interpretation on occurrences and upon the actions of others. In everyday life, many situations arise in which the wrong impression or interpretation can take place.

It is sometimes easy to misinterpret notices, or the words which appear in newspaper headlines. Imagine, for example, that you were a foreigner with only a reasonable grasp of English, and you saw the following signs:

O.H.P. 1 •In the London Underground ...
[Does that mean that, if you don't have a dog, you may not travel on the escalator?]

O.H.P. 2 (•Outside a Hospital ...), **O.H.P. 3** (•On a Bus ...), **O.H.P. 4** (•Some examples of Newspaper Headlines ...)

In the same way, when dealing with people, it is so important that we do not jump to conclusions ...

THE TICKET COLLECTOR

One Friday a Ticket-Collector was checking tickets on the London to Newcastle train and entered the First Class compartment. There he asked to see the ticket of an old man who was shabbily dressed in an old tweed suit. The old man couldn't find his ticket, and started to search through two old battered suitcases. The Ticket-Collector watched the old man and thought he had come across someone who should be in the Second Class area, where single tickets were £60, rather than the First Class area, where a single ticket cost £90. Just as he was about to ask him to move out, the old man found his ticket in one of the many little pockets of his suit.

The Ticket-Collector felt a pang of guilt because he had judged the man only on his appearance. When the train got to Newcastle he noticed the old man standing on the platform with two heavy suitcases, and so he called a Porter to take his cases to a taxi for him. Just as the Porter was about to pick up the cases, he moved away to pick up the case of a very well-dressed lady and take her by the arm to the taxi.

The Ticket-Collector was taken aback that the Porter should avoid the old man and choose someone who looked richer. To make up for what he had done on the train, he himself picked the old man's cases up and took them to the taxi. The old man thanked him, gave him a £20 note tip, and said:

"What I would like you to do is go and find that Porter and say to him that if he had not been only too ready to judge me because of my clothes, then the £20 would have been his." The Ticket-Collector found the Porter and did as he had been asked.

The Porter listened quietly, then said: "Each Friday that old lady, who is nearly blind and unsafe on her feet, comes up from Leeds, to visit her daughter, who is seriously ill in Newcastle General Hospital. One of us Porters always looks after her since she had a bad fall last winter - and we have never taken a penny!"

THE BEST INTERPRETATION

NEWCASTLE UNITED

A man went into a second-hand bookshop in Newcastle, and came across a volume, with a cover emblazoned with black and white stripes, entitled "Newcastle United". Because he was a fanatical Newcastle United Football supporter, he grabbed it from the shelf, and paid the necessary sum of money to the cashier. He couldn't wait to get home to read about his favourite team, but when he opened up the book, he found it was a history of how Newcastle had united together in the 19th Century to form Newcastle City Council.

O.H.P. 5

Just another example which goes to show that, far too easily, people are prepared to jump to the wrong conclusion.

The question is - How can this basic Gospel value of not making rash judgements be applied to our own lives in School and outside of School? Daily examples abound ...

- If, for example, somebody passes you on the corridor and does not say "Hello!" or "Good morning!" then is it fair to assume that they are ignoring you? Quite simply, they might be short-sighted, have lost their contact lenses, or they might have been so engrossed in some personal thoughts that they were oblivious to your presence.

- If someone fails to turn up to meet you outside the disco, it might well be because there has been a crisis at home - the budgie has died, or they may have had an accident.

- If someone doesn't telephone you, perhaps it is because they cannot get on the phone because their Mother or Father is using it - surprisingly, Parents are allowed to use the phone from time to time!

CONCLUSION

Always, then, think the best before considering the worst!

THE BEST INTERPRETATION

SCRIPTURE READING

St. Luke, Chapter 18 : verses 9-14

Jesus also told this parable to people who were sure of their own goodness and despised everybody else.

"Once there were two men who went up to the Temple to pray: one was a Pharisee, the other a Tax Collector.

"The Pharisee stood apart by himself and prayed: 'i thank You that I am not like that Tax Collector over there. I fast two days a week, and I give you a tenth of all my income.'

"But the Tax Collector stood at a distance, and would not even raise his face to Heaven, but beat on his breast and said: 'God, have pity on me, a sinner!'"

"I tell you," said Jesus, "The Tax Collector, and not the Pharisee, was in the right with God when he went home."

THE BEST INTERPRETATION
MATERIAL FOR O.H.P.

O.H.P. 1

In the London Underground ...

DOGS MUST BE CARRIED ON THE ESCALATORS

O.H.P. 2

Outside a Hospital ...

GUARD DOGS OPERATING

O.H.P. 3

On a Bus ...

PASSENGERS ALIGHT AT BOTH ENDS

O.H.P. 4

Newspaper Headlines ...

BABIES FLOOD HOSPITALS

MAN FOUND DEAD IN CEMETERY

ESCAPED LEOPARD  BELIEVED SPOTTED

O.H.P. 5

NEWCASTLE UNITED

THE BEST INTERPRETATION

SUGGESTED RESOURCES ...

THE PICTURES
(OVERHEAD PROJECTOR)

- Miscellaneous Notices, Signs and Headlines
- "Newcastle United" Cover

THE MUSIC

- "He Ain't Heavy - He's My Brother" - The Hollies
- "Let Your Love Flow" - Bellamy Brothers
- "A Boy Named Sue" - Johnny Cash
- "Think It Over" - The Crickets
- "People Are People" - Depeche Mode
- "Ideal World" - The Christians
- "Bad Boy" - Wham
- "Coward of the County" - Kenny Rogers

THE WORDS

SCRIPTURE READING

St. Luke, Chapter 18: verses 9-14

THE TRAGEDY OF REJECTION

INTRODUCTION ...

John Powell once said that there are two potential tragedies in life - one is to go through life without loving, and the second is not to express love and affection for those who love us.

O.H.P. 1 THE STORY OF THE FISH

At the university of California, Scientists performed an experiment. They placed a fish - a pike - in a glass tank, and they fed it well. It thrived and it appeared as happy as any fish can be judged to appear in such circumstances. They used to put a plate of food down on the floor of the tank, and each time it came and ate it. They then placed a glass partition in the tank and started to place the plate of food on the side of the partition away from the fish. The fish did not realise the partition was there, and time and time again it swam down to collect the food, only to bash into the glass. Eventually it would swim towards the food, and just before it made contact, it would veer away.

They then removed the partition and put the food in the normal place. The fish would swim towards it but, afraid to run into something solid, would swerve away before it got to the plate. Time after time this happened and nothing could induce the pike to eat. In spite of putting food elsewhere, the damage had been done, and ultimately the fish died from malnutrition.

THE TRAGEDY OF REJECTION

CONCLUSION

Despite the fact that finally there was food all around it, the pike had been hurt so many times that it could not bring itself to eat. The fish could well represent mankind. We all need, want and respond to love, kindness and encouragement. We all are destroyed by rejection, ridicule and hostility. It was a silly, or perhaps a very insensitive and hardened, individual who wrote: *"Sticks and stones may break my bones, but calling will not hurt me."* The fact is that harsh words, as well as actions, *do* hurt, and inflict untold damage - a process which in life is normally described as bullying.

The unfortunate reality is that we live in a culture which is disinclined to demonstrate tenderness and is slow in coming forward to express its feelings. Many would like to show their love and affection, but are too shy shy or worried about being rejected to convey that fondness and warmth. But such a demonstration can mean so much to so many.

We need to make better friends of our friends, express affection, appreciation and kinship frequently and readily. So thank those who love you, and tell them that you love them.

SCRIPTURE READING
1 Corinthians, Chapter 13 : verses 1-7

I may be able to speak the languages of men and even of angels, but if I have no love, my speech is no more than a noisy gong or a clanging bell. I may have the gift of inspired preaching; I may have all knowledge, and understand all secrets; I may have all the faith needed to move mountains - but if I have no love, I am nothing. I may give away everything I have, and even give up my body to be burnt - but if I have no love, this does me no good.

Love is patient and kind; it is not jealous or conceited or proud; love is not ill-mannered or selfish or irritable; love does not keep a record of wrongs; love is not happy with evil, but is happy with the truth. Love never gives up; and its faith, hope, and patience never fail.

THE TRAGEDY OF REJECTION

MATERIAL FOR O.H.P.

O.H.P. 1

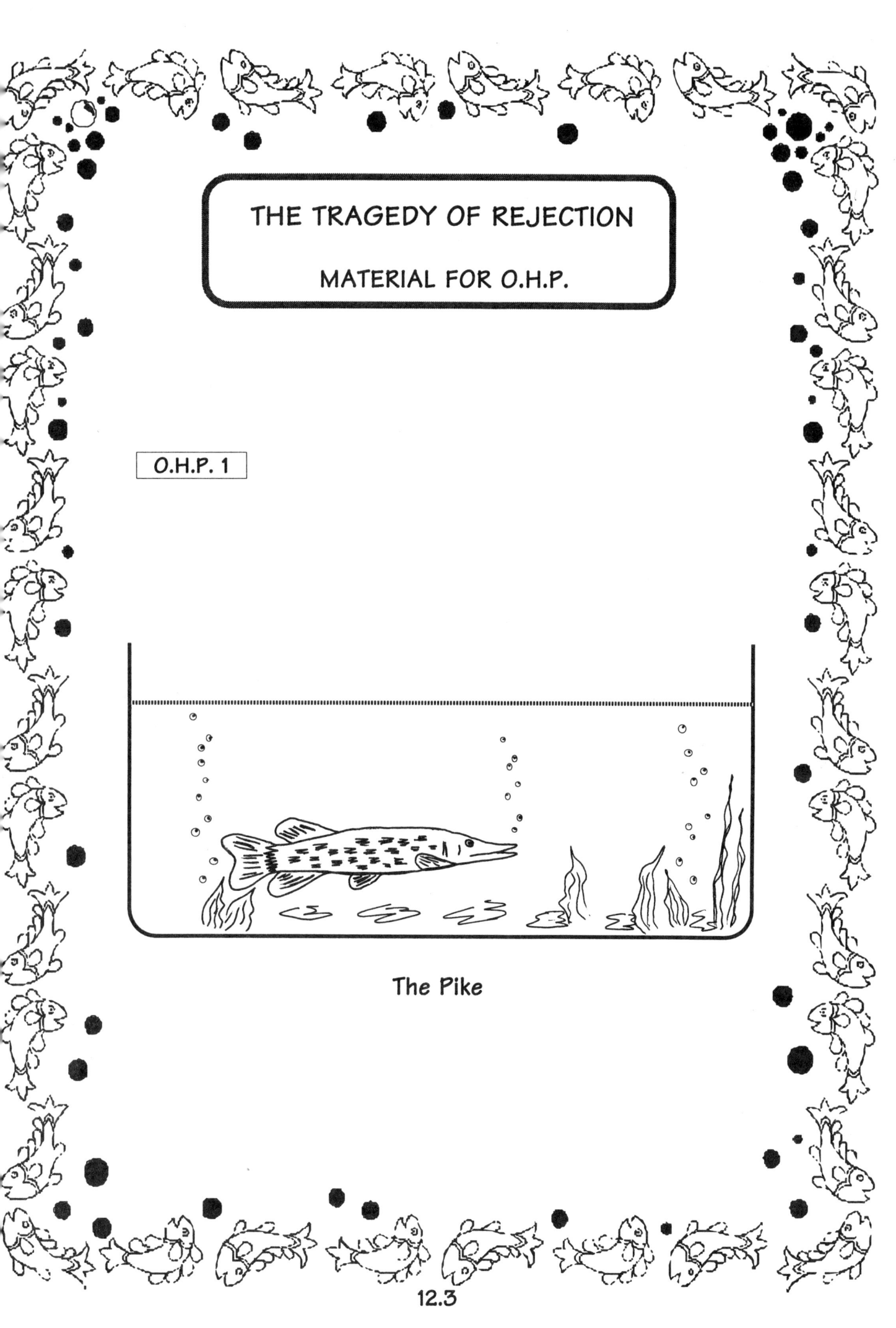

The Pike

THE TRAGEDY OF REJECTION

SUGGESTED RESOURCES ...

THE PICTURES
(OVERHEAD PROJECTOR)

- Fish in Tank

THE MUSIC

- "Thank You For The Days" - Kirsty MacColl
- "Another Day In Paradise" - Phil Collins
- "Everybody Hurts" - R.E.M.
- "Justice" - Alan Price
- "The First Cut Is The Deepest" - Cat Stevens
- "Help!" - The Beatles
- "All You Need Is Love" - The Beatles
- "Let Your Love Flow" - Bellamy Brothers
- "Streets Of London" - Ralph McTell
- "Bridge Over Troubled Water" - Simon and Garfunkel
- "Without Love You Are Nothing" - Larry Norman
- "Short People" - Randy Newman

THE WORDS

SCRIPTURE READING

1 Corinthians, Chapter 13 : verses 1-7

THE HUMAN WILL AND SPIRIT

INTRODUCTION ...

In October 1995, much was made of the way Jaymee Bowen - "Child B" as she was described initially to preserve her anonymity - was still alive and prospering even though National Health doctors had refused her treatment for advanced leukæmia on the grounds that her case was hopeless. By October she should have been dead. Her Father refused to accept the decision of the doctors and his persistence in looking for help paid off. When Jaymee was asked if she had any message she would like to pass on to people who might find themselves in a similar position, she said: "While there is the slightest bit life, never give up hope."

It is extraordinary how many times newspapers carry reports of events and circumstances in which it has appeared that someone was facing certain death and then luck or sheer determination and persistence has intervened to save them.

Two incidents from 1995 would serve to illustrate the point ...

Skoda Survival

Kevin Slauter, who came from Brighton, one day was driving his Skoda car along the coast road above the cliffs near his home and tried to overtake a slow-moving lorry. The car ran out of control, and before he knew it, he had crashed through a safety fence, over a grass verge, headlong over a sheer cliff-face, and had plunged 150 feet down to the beach.

Believe it or not, the only thing which saved him was the fact that he was driving a Skoda car! The engine was in the back and cushioned him from the full impact. He broke his shoulder, collar-bone, pelvis and ribs, but is expected to make a full recovery.

Who would believe it of a Skoda, the car which is the butt of many a comedian's jokes?

Question : "What is the difference between a double glazing salesman and a Skoda car?"
Answer : "You can close the door on a double glazing salesman!"

or

Question: What do you call a Skoda with a sun-roof?
Answer: A skip!

THE HUMAN WILL AND SPIRIT

Los Angeles Earthquake   O.H.P. 1

A similar story, and one in which luck played its part in the survival of someone, was when, in January of 1995, a man by the name of David Farley was driving his station-wagon along Inter-State Road 5, and found himself on top of a bridge when a severe earthquake struck. A few feet in front of him there opened up a huge split in the road, with a 75-foot drop. 50 yards behind him a small crack had appeared. David jumped out of the wagon, ran back towards the small crack, and with two other drivers, jumped over it. Within seconds, the crack had stretched to over 20 yards and that section of the bridge collapsed in a heap of rubble.

In both of these stories, men had survived because of good fortune. Lady Luck had shone upon them.

THE HUMAN SPIRIT

However, from time to time you do come across stories where people survive and manage to continue to live, not because they are lucky, but because they have discovered within themselves, in dangerous and hazardous situations, the will and the desire to survive despite all of the odds being stacked against them. There is, for example, the story of a girl who was called ...

... Juliane Keopte

Juliane was 17 in 1974, when she flew with her mother to Peru to see her father, who was working there. When they were over the jungle in Peru, the plane in which they were travelling broke up in mid-air. The next thing Juliane remembers is that she found herself half-way up a tree, still strapped in her seat, and completely alone. Her mother's empty seat was stuck in the tree beside her, but no other remains of the plane were in sight.

O.H.P. 2

THE HUMAN WILL AND SPIRIT

Juliane Keopte (Continued)

Here then was this young girl of 17, completely alone in the jungle. The only sound in the dense undergrowth was the sound of birds and strange noises which she had never heard before. Her face battered and bruised, stiff from head to toe, and for some reason barely able to see, she climbed down from the tree, and, bare-footed, she began to walk, hopefully towards some centre of habitation. The shoes which she had been wearing had come off in the crash and had disappeared. She had, then, no choice but to make her way bare-foot through the undergrowth. After walking for a couple of hours, she came to a small stream, and decided to follow its flow in the hope that it would join up with a large river. After two days' travelling, she did eventually come to a much bigger river. By this time her feet were cut and bruised, and she found it almost impossible to bear the agony of putting her weight on them. To make matters worse, she had been bitten by a series of insects and mosquitoes, and, as she found later, worms had begun to grow under her skin. In total, for ten days she forced herself on, hardly knowing what she was doing. Her only nourishment was a small Christmas cake which she had saved in her pocket from the aeroplane. Leeches sucked her blood as they clung to her, and she became so exhausted that she had to enter the stream and allow the current to carry her down-river, swimming as best she could. Even the thought of the piranha fish, which are attracted by blood, did not put her off. On the tenth day, she eventually came to a mud hut and managed to lie down, for the first time in ten nights, on some sacking which she found within the hut. On the next day she came face to face with one of the Peruvian native women, who shrieked with horror on seeing her face utterly distorted by insect bites, sun, and the ravages of the jungle.

Juliane is German, and is now fully recovered, 20 years later, and lives in Munich. What drove her on, she says, was the thought that she must see her father, who, she felt, would have been unable to take the death of both herself and her mother.

Such a story shows the remarkable spirit which can be engendered within human beings when they feel they really must survive.

THE HUMAN WILL AND SPIRIT

O.H.P. 3

The Case of Pedro de Serrano, 1540

At the end of the day, no matter how much spirit, endurance, hope and desire you may have for survival, you still require the basic ingredients of food, water, and, in terrible conditions, shelter to sustain you in your efforts.

In 1540, a man by the name of Pedro de Serrano was wrecked on a desert island. This wasn't the type of desert island you read about in Robinson Crusoe, where there was clear water, lush vegetation, coconut trees, and plenty of shade. Pedro found himself on an island which was just a long bank of sand. There was no food, no water, and the sun blazed down - conditions in which certain and slow death seemed assured.

Yet Pedro survived. He hunted for cockles, which he ate raw. For moisture, he caught a turtle and drank its blood. He collected drift-wood, but there were no pebbles or stones to strike together to make fire, and so he swam down and brought two up from the sea-bed. He survived in this way for three years.

And then, one day, great joy! He saw in the distance a ship approaching, with one survivor on board, who waved to him. However, as the boat was coming in towards the island, tragedy struck. It smashed against the rocks as it approached the beach, and the only things that were left were the survivor and drift-wood.

They survived another four years together before being picked up by a passing merchant ship. During that time, they continued to live off cockles, raw fish and rain-water (which they collected within their clothes), and turtle blood. From time to time there were differences between them: they quarrelled and they fought, even dividing up the island at one stage between the two of them. However, they always made it up, became friends, and afterwards met each year to celebrate the anniversary of their rescue from their desert island.

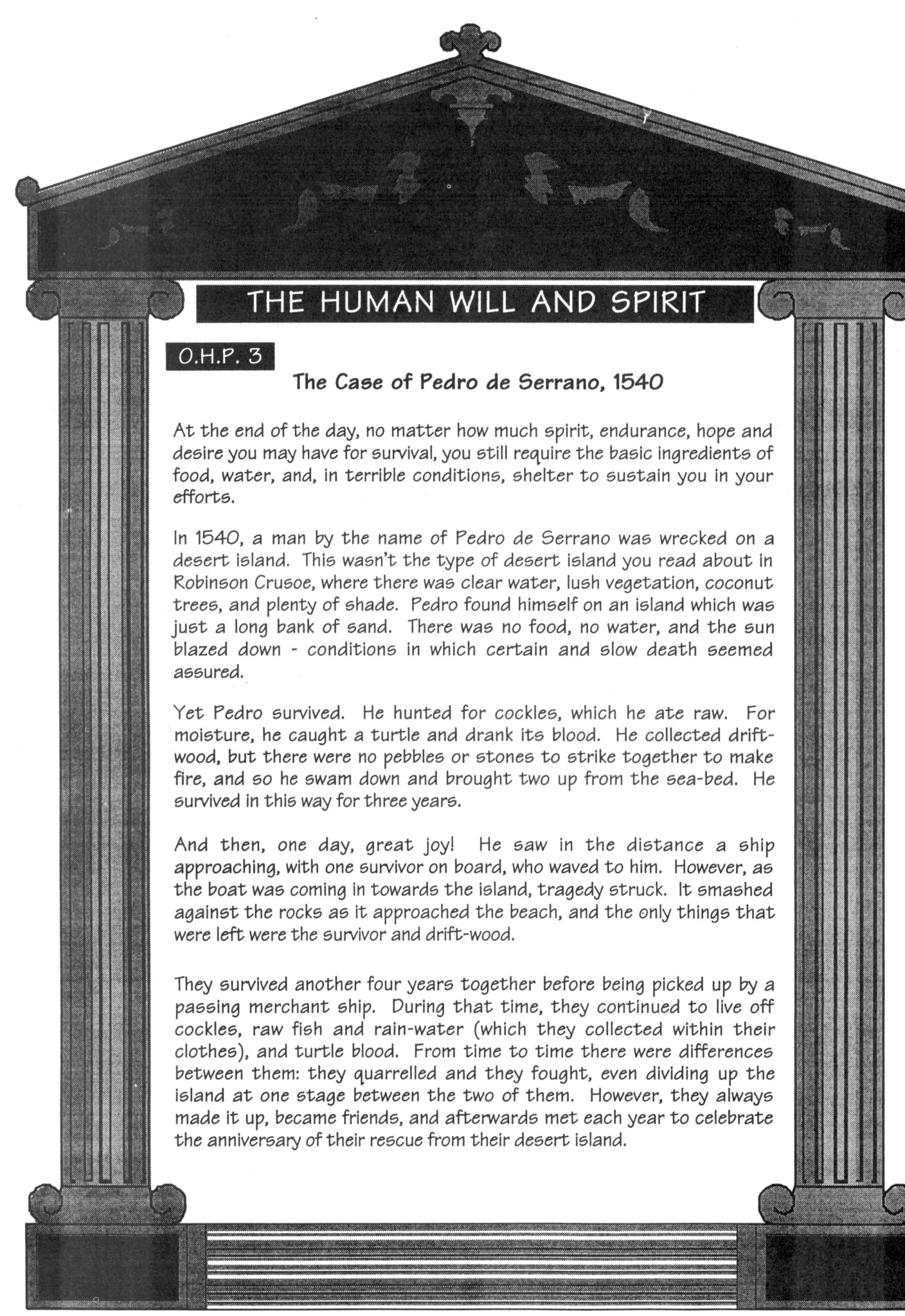

THE HUMAN WILL AND SPIRIT

CONCLUSION

THE MESSAGE OF THESE STORIES

When called upon, man has an indomitable will and desire to survive. It would seem that no matter what the circumstances, no matter how desperate people are, if they do not despair and do not abandon hope, it is possible to overcome almost certain death. The message is that, however grave the circumstances and however much there is the temptation to give up, we all have the capacity to meet with problems and strive to triumph. Man has hidden depths and inner strengths which should never be under-estimated.

SCRIPTURE READING

James, Chapter 1: verses 2-4

My brothers, consider yourselves fortunate when all kinds of trial come your way, for you know that when your faith succeeds in facing such trials, the result is the ability to endure. Make sure that your endurance carries you all the way without failing, so that you may be perfect and complete, lacking nothing.

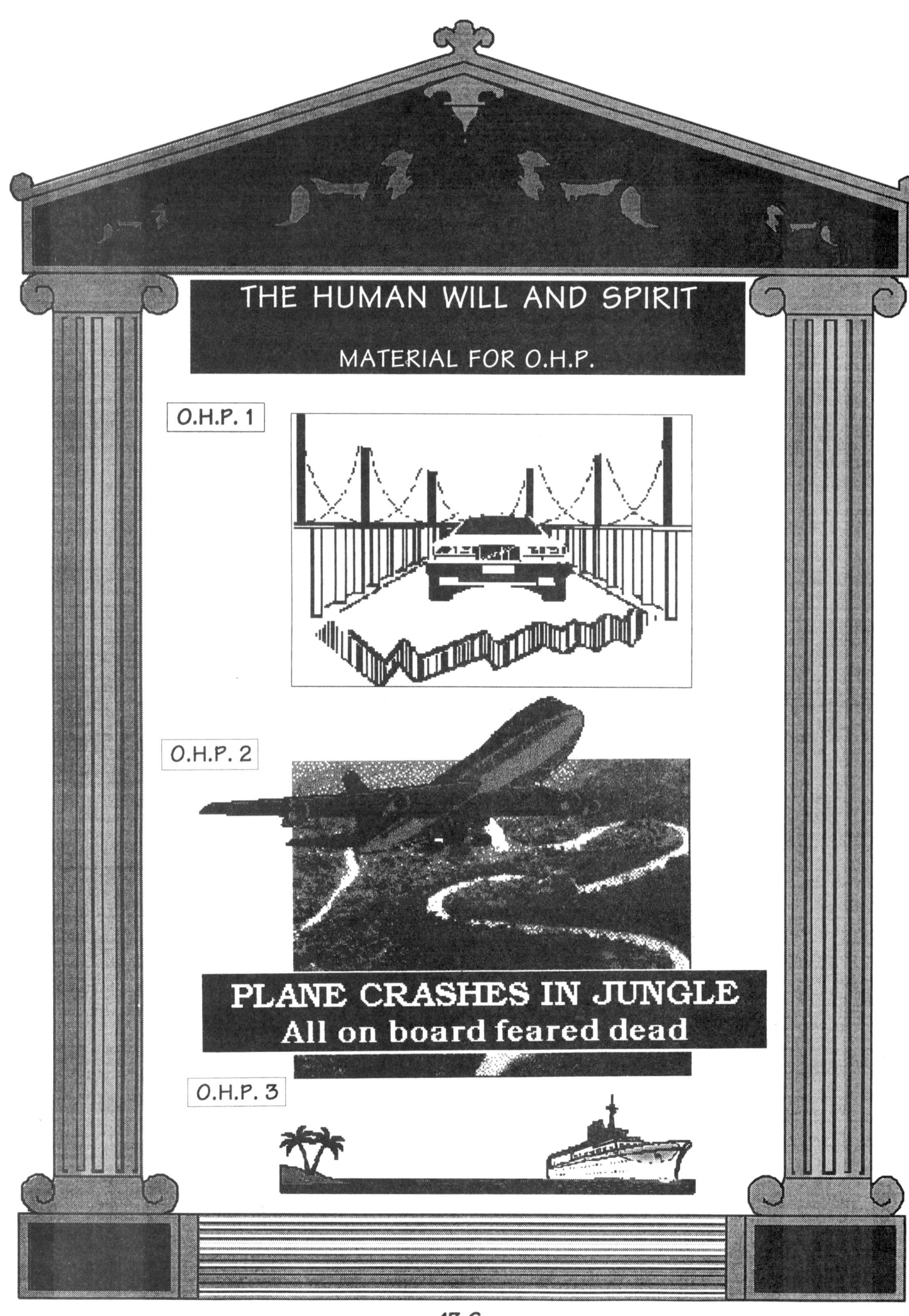

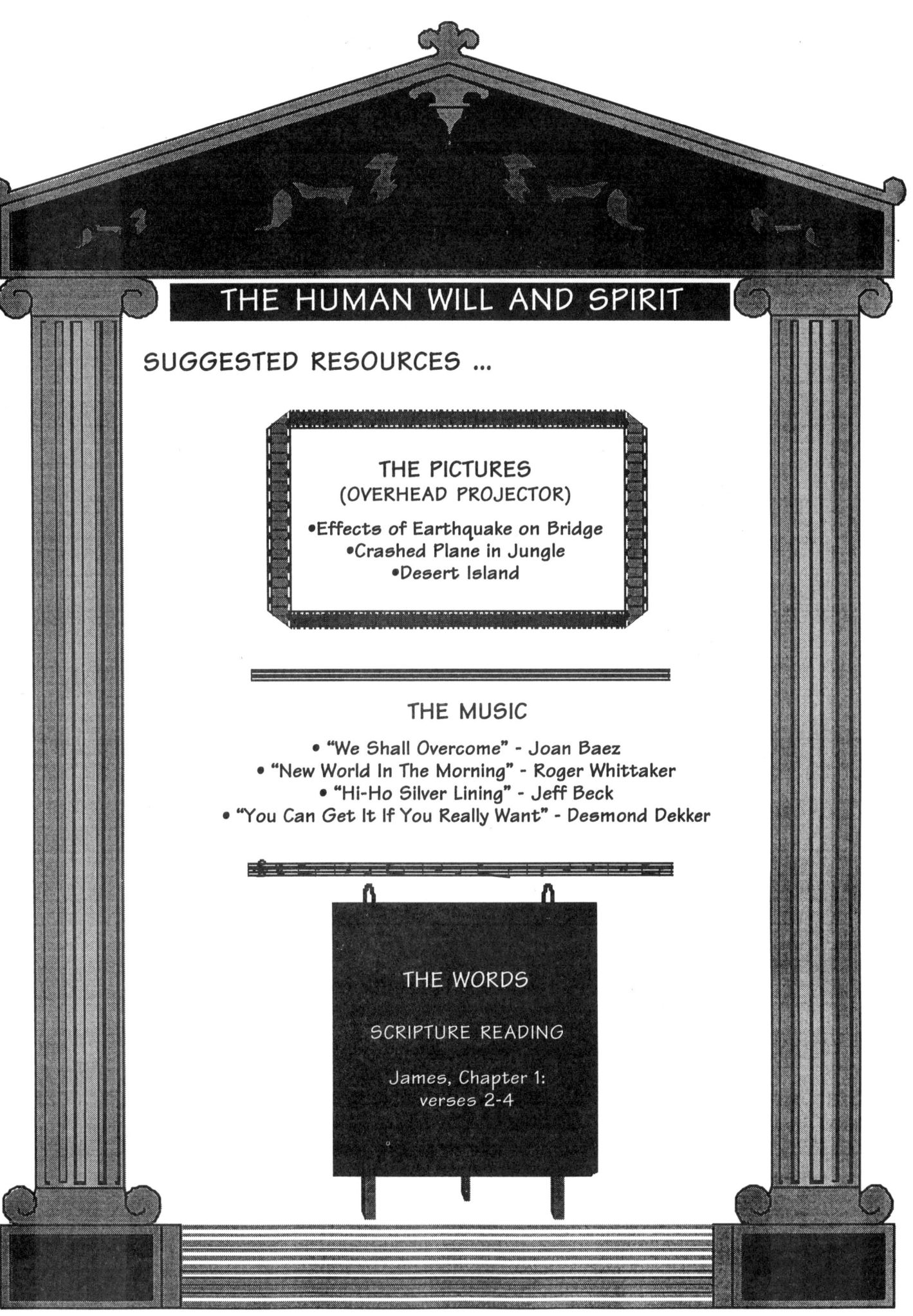

YOUNG PEOPLE: DO TIMES REALLY CHANGE?

INTRODUCTION ...

The relationship between the old and the young, between parents and children, is inevitably strained as children grow older and begin to assert their individuality. Happy and unique indeed is the family which exists in perfect harmony - a situation as rare as a sizeable win on the Lottery!

HELPFUL OBSERVATIONS?

There appears to exist a reservoir of common expressions, based on their own youthful experiences, which parents have a tendency to use in their efforts to cajole young members of their families to make the most of their opportunities in life. When examples of these (*see below*) are mentioned to a group of pupils, their knowing grins reveal that very many have been the victims of such well-meaning campaigns. The only trouble is that such 'bons mots' have a propensity to lead to youthful irritability and resentment. They frequently start with the phrase ...

When I was your age ...   O.H.P. 1

or ...   O.H.P. 2

Other oft-used but potentially inflammatory comments in this context are:

- As long as you live in my house ...
- I'm only doing this for your own good
- Some day you'll thank me
- I don't want to hear any more about it
- How many times have I told you ...?
- This is hurting me more than it's going to hurt you;
  apropos of which reassurance -

  (Father, chancing to chastise
  His indignant daughter Sue,
  Said: "I hope you realise
  That this hurts me more than you."

  Susan ceased to roar;
  "If that's really true,:said she,
  "I can stand a good deal more;
  Pray go on , and don't mind me."

  - Harry Graham,
  Ruthless Rhymes 1899)

YOUNG PEOPLE: DO TIMES REALLY CHANGE?

Such observations, valid though they may be, do not help in building up an understanding dialogue between individuals of different generations. Such remarks antagonised the same adults when they were younger.

Likewise such statements on the part of young people as ...

- *This is the 1990s, you know*
- *Just because you're past it*
- *Times have changed since the First World War*
- *All my friends can/have ...*

`O.H.P. 3`

... are not destined to help the profferer of such pronouncements be a prime candidate for the Nobel Peace Prize.

BLASTS FROM THE PAST

Here are two extracts commenting on the young. It is interesting to try and guess when they were written:

`O.H.P. 4`   `O.H.P. 5`

Though one would be forgiven if one thought that these were from modern times. Extract 1 was written by the poet Hesiod who lived in Greece in the 8th Century, and Extract 2 by Peter the Monk in the 13th Century.

CONCLUSION

The relationship between the old and the young, between fathers and mothers and daughters and sons, has been a problem since the beginning of time. There has been, and always will be, friction and sources of conflict in which reasonableness and adjustments in attitude and approach need to be made. To find solutions is never easy. The most people can do is to make every effort to see the other's point of view and appreciate that parents and relatives give advice with the best of intentions and without malice. But human nature being what it is, they - like all of us - can easily make mistakes.

Parents and Grandchildren have chosen to have children of their own and therefore do not fall into that category of mankind who are out to cause as much hassle for their children as they can - a category perhaps best exemplified by the American comic actor, W. C. Fields who has been attributed with uttering: "Anybody who hates children and dogs can't be all bad."

As parents, young people themselves would never accept the attractive but impractical suggestion given by Harry S. Truman in 1955:

> *"I have found that the best way to give advice to your children is to find out what they want and then advise them to do it."*

YOUNG PEOPLE: DO TIMES REALLY CHANGE?

SCRIPTURE READING

St. Mark, Chapter 10: verses 13-16

Some people brought children to Jesus for Him to place His Hands on them, but the Disciples scolded the people. When Jesus noticed this, He was angry, and said to His Disciples: "Let the children come to Me, and do not stop them, because the Kingdom of God belongs to such as these. I assure you that whoever does not receive the Kingdom of God like a child will never enter it." Then He took the children in His Arms, placed His Hands on each of them, and blessed them.

YOUNG PEOPLE: DO TIMES REALLY CHANGE?

MATERIAL FOR O.H.P.

O.H.P. 1

WHEN I WAS YOUR AGE ...

- ... We had to eat what we were given
- ... We would never have dared say that to our parents
- ... We showed respect for our elders
- ... We had to be in no later than 7 o'clock at your age
- ... We had to make our own entertainment
- ... We never had the same chances as you have had
- ... We had to be happy with two days at Blackpool
- ... We were happy with a tangerine and some walnuts for Christmas
- ... We were so poor as children that one day my mother gave me a button and said: "Run next door and ask Mrs. Dodds to put a shirt on that for you!"

O.H.P. 2

- We were so poor that as a lad I couldn't go outside till I was three because I had no clothes. Then one day my Father went to a jumble sale and bought a cap. Only then could I look out of the window.

O.H.P. 3

- **This is the 1990s, you know**
- **Just because you're past it**
- **Times have changed since the First World War**
- **All my friends can/have ...**

YOUNG PEOPLE: DO TIMES REALLY CHANGE?

MATERIAL FOR O.H.P.
(Continued)

O.H.P. 4

Extract 1 ...

"When I was a boy, we were taught to be discreet and respectful of our elders, but the present youth are exceedingly impatient of restraint. They have detestable manners, take no notice of authority, and have no respect for their elders. What sort of creatures will they be when they grow up?"

O.H.P. 5

Extract 2 ...

"The young people of today think of nothing and nobody but themselves. They have no reverence for parents or old age. They talk as if they alone know everything."

O.H.P. 6

"I have found that the best way to give advice to your children is to find out what they want and then advise them to do it."

YOUNG PEOPLE: DO TIMES REALLY CHANGE?

SUGGESTED RESOURCES ...

THE PICTURES
(OVERHEAD PROJECTOR)

- Miscellaneous quotations on theme "When I was your age ..."

THE MUSIC

- "Father and Son" - Cat Stevens
- "On The Road To Find Out" - Cat Stevens
- "Oh, Very Young" - Cat Stevens
- "Top Of The World" - The Carpenters
- "Walk Of Life" - Dire Straits
- "Shades Of Grey" - The Monkees
- "Turn, Turn, Turn" - The Byrds
- "When The Going Gets Tough, The Tough Get Going" - Billy Ocean

THE WORDS

SCRIPTURE READING

St. Mark, Chapter 10: verses 13-16

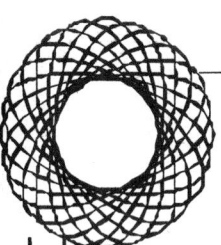  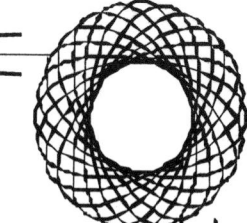

PEACE

INTRODUCTION ...

A sentence from the famous prayer of St. Francis of Assisi is: "Make me an instrument of Your Peace." Frequently it is something we forget, and instead we are instruments of discord and disharmony. Rather than being the victims, we become the perpetrators.

STORY

We might read in amazement the case of the Grimsby motorist so incensed by being "tooted" to move over from the middle of the road, that he followed the perceived wrong-doer home and gave him a sound thrashing for his impertinence. "Road Rage" had taken hold of him and the transformation from docility to fury had been effected. The character references in Court which alluded to his tranquillity of temperament, caring parent-hood and dedication as a foreman ambulance-man did not rescue him from the shame or the sack.

How easy it seems to be for "Road Rage" to take a grip. Normally sensible men and women lose their tempers when they are overtaken, or someone cuts marginally in front of them.

The same insanity appears to affect individuals as they wait in queues.

Witness the scene in an ASDA supermarket when a man inadvertently joined the front, rather than the back, of the queue at the bread counter and was served by a rushed and pressurised assistant who had not realised it was not his turn. An obviously vengeful and angry house-wife, having been served her two crusty French sticks, hastened after the culprit, and beat him about the head with the aforementioned sticks, reducing them to crumbs in the "Fruit and Vegetable" aisle.

Experts explain the behaviour as being a result of today's high pressure World, the stress of day-to-day living coupled with some perceived slight on the road or elsewhere, and suggest that is enough to send even the most mild-mannered individual over the edge.

CONCLUSION

To feel entitled to exact retribution unreasonably because of a personal problem or a perceived slight is unjustified. The fact that a flat tyre has made us late for work, or the goldfish has passed on, is not an excuse for temper tantrums and expressions of hostility. It is well to remember the observation: "The mass of men lead lives of quiet desperation." It is by understanding the lives of others that we can make lives more peaceful, and become "instruments" of peace.

PEACE

PRAYER

Help us to live at peace with others;
To keep from saying hurtful words;
To stop doing anything which will cause bad feeling;
To control our tempers when we become angry;
To always put the best interpretation on people's actions;
To forgive those who hurt us in word or deed.
Amen

SCRIPTURE READING

Hebrews, Chapter 12:
verses 14-15

Try and be at peace with everyone, and try to live a holy life, because no-one will see the Lord without it. Guard against turning back from the Grace of God. Let no-one become like a bitter plant that grows up and causes many troubles with its poison.

PEACE

SUGGESTED RESOURCES ...

THE PICTURES
(OVERHEAD PROJECTOR)

- Road Rage
- Woman beating man over head with French stick

THE MUSIC

- "Peace Train" - Cat Stevens
- "Peace Will Come" - Tom Paxton
- "There's A Kind Of Hush (All Over The World)" - The Carpenters
- "From A Distance" - Nancy Quin
- "If I Had A Hammer" - Trini Lopez
- "Caravan Of Love" - The Housemartins
- "Let Your Love Flow" - Bellamy Brothers
- "My Sweet Lord" - George Harrison
- "Last Night I Had The Strangest Dream" - Simon and Garfunkel

THE WORDS

SCRIPTURE READING

Hebrews, Chapter 12: verses 14-15

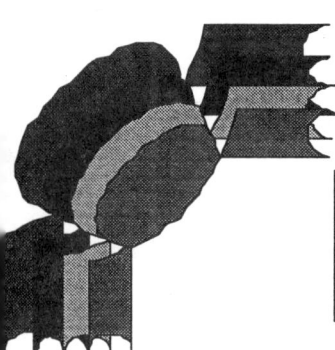

THE SADNESS AND THE HOPE OF DEATH

INTRODUCTION ...

Death brings with it for those who have loved and are left behind an agony and torment which only those who mourn can fully appreciate. That grief, akin to despair which can crush the very mind, is part of the process of death and bereavement through which we must travel along with the memories, the farewells and the hope.

THE PAIN

When someone dies who has been close to us, someone we have loved, it brings with it a sorrow and a pain which cannot be described until it has been experienced. As Christians we may believe in the Resurrection when we shall all be together but in mourning that can seem a long way off at some indefinite time in the future. No-one can prepare us for the anguish and the reality of death.

The suffering is deep no matter how old the deceased may be, but if the person is young then it appears to be a double tragedy. It is particularly hard to bear and searing on the heart when someone is snatched away in the full bloom of youth, with dreams unfulfilled and beauty and opportunity lost forever.

When someone dies, be they mother, father, brother, sister, child or friend, you are left with an acute awareness of their uniqueness and their irreplaceability.

What we must remember is that the pain of parting is the price we pay for love.

It should help to persuade us how important it is that we should always bid farewell to those we love the way we would wish to be remembered or we would like them to remember us. To leave someone unforgiving or in bitterness is something we could well regret for the rest of our lives.

It is a thought expressed in this observation from Gwyn Thomas:

> *"I remember those happy days, and often wish I could speak into the ears of the dead the gratitude which was due to them in life and so ill-returned."*

If there is someone you love and appreciate, then **tell** them. You may never get the chance to do so again.

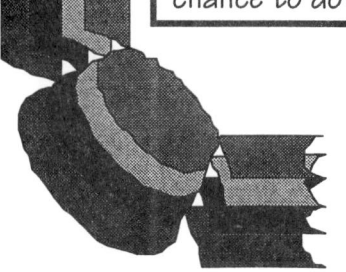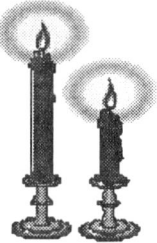

THE SADNESS AND THE HOPE OF DEATH

THE MEMORIES

When someone dies, then we must treasure their memories, because our lives will have been touched in unique ways by the deceased. We must hold up and offer those memories, which will remain with us in spirit.

THE FAREWELL

It is at the funeral service that we release the person physically but retain their spirit.

As Christians, we believe there will come a time when we shall meet with those deceased again, and these sentiments are echoed throughout the Christian services for those who have died.

A PRAYER OF HOPE O.H.P. 1

"Death is nothing at all ... I have only slipped away into the next room ... I am I and you are you ... whatever we were to each other, that we are still. Call me by my own familiar name, speak to me in the easy way you always used to. Put no difference into your tone; wear no forced air of solemnity or sorrow. Laugh as we always laughed at the little jokes we enjoyed together. Play, smile, think of me, pray for me. Let my name be ever the household word that it always was. Let it be spoken without effect, without the ghost of a shadow on it. Life means all that it ever meant. It is the same as it ever was; there is absolutely unbroken continuity. What is death but a negligible accident? Why should I be put out of mind because I am out of sight? I am but waiting for you, for an interval, somewhere very near, just around the corner ... All is well."

THE RAINBOW O.H.P. 2

In the Summer of 1994 a Christian convention was held in Canada on the theme 'The Rainbow', which has come to represent "Resurrection." At the final ceremony of the gathering, a young couple requested the opportunity to come forward and tell their story to the assembled 7,000. A young mother told how, a few months previously, her son of 11 had died of cancer. After the funeral, the close family had gathered in the home and were having a cup of tea. The mother told how she felt completely depressed and could not get her son out of her mind, worrying whether he was at peace.

There was a knock on the door, and it was one of their neighbours telling them to go to the window and look outside. When they did so, there in the sky was the most perfect of rainbows (the symbol of the Resurrection) which had appeared apparently without any climatic intervention. As she looked at the rainbow, she distinctly heard her son's voice telling her not to worry and that he was happy and at rest. He went on to say that, to prove she was not imagining what she was hearing, an equally perfect rainbow would appear in exactly the same place at exactly the same time the following day.

Next day, the whole family and friends gathered, and there in the sky, at exactly the time and the place predicted, was the most perfect of rainbows.

THE SADNESS AND THE HOPE OF DEATH

LIFE AFTER DEATH

It is interesting to read some of the information contained in a book recently published by Peter and Elizabeth Fenwick, which is entitled: "The Truth in the Light." This is a meticulous analysis of responses from questionnaires involving 300 people whose "near-death experiences" are investigated. These experiences are assessed not in purely spiritual or religious terms, but as something "mystical".

It was obviously very difficult for all who responded to elucidate verbally or in writing their experiences, but where they did manage to find the words, as the authors say:

> *"A surprisingly uniform vision of paradise emerges. It is a picture of a heavenly countryside where there may be brilliantly coloured birds and flowers, wonderful scents, heavenly music, friends or relatives who have died and sometimes, especially in the case of children, living friends as well."*

A substantial number amongst the 300 describe how they had reached their near-death experience (or N.D.E.) by travelling through a tunnel with a warm and welcoming bright light at the end of it.

What was a common feature was that, for these 300, the prospect of death held no fear or dread whatsoever.

THE SADNESS AND THE HOPE OF DEATH
MATERIAL FOR O.H.P.

O.H.P. 1

"DEATH IS NOTHING AT ALL . . . I HAVE ONLY SLIPPED AWAY INTO THE NEXT ROOM . . . I AM I AND YOU ARE YOU . . . WHATEVER WE WERE TO EACH OTHER, THAT WE ARE STILL. CALL ME BY MY OWN FAMILIAR NAME, SPEAK TO ME IN THE EASY WAY YOU ALWAYS USED TO. PUT NO DIFFERENCE INTO YOUR TONE; WEAR NO FORCED AIR OF SOLEMNITY OR SORROW. LAUGH AS WE ALWAYS LAUGHED AT THE LITTLE JOKES WE ENJOYED TOGETHER. PLAY, SMILE, THINK OF ME, PRAY FOR ME. LET MY NAME BE EVER THE HOUSEHOLD WORD THAT IT ALWAYS WAS. LET IT BE SPOKEN WITHOUT EFFECT, WITHOUT THE GHOST OF A SHADOW ON IT. LIFE MEANS ALL THAT IT EVER MEANT. IT IS THE SAME AS IT EVER WAS; THERE IS ABSOLUTELY UNBROKEN CONTINUITY. WHAT IS DEATH BUT A NEGLIGIBLE ACCIDENT? WHY SHOULD I BE PUT OUT OF MIND BECAUSE I AM OUT OF SIGHT? I AM BUT WAITING FOR YOU, FOR AN INTERVAL, SOMEWHERE VERY NEAR, JUST AROUND THE CORNER . . . ALL IS WELL."

O.H.P. 2

THE SADNESS AND THE HOPE OF DEATH

SUGGESTED RESOURCES ...

THE PICTURES
(OVERHEAD PROJECTOR)

- "Death Is Nothing At All ..."
- A Rainbow

THE MUSIC

- "Tears In Heaven" - Eric Clapton
- "Seasons In The Sun" - Terry Jacks
- "No Woman, No Cry" - Boney M
- "Thank You For the Days" - Kirsty MacColl
- "Stairway To Heaven" - Led Zeppelin
- "Wreck On The Highway" - Bruce Springsteen
- "Those Were The Days Of Our Lives" - Queen

THE WORDS

SCRIPTURE READING

St. John, Chapter 11: verses 20-25
(The Death of Lazarus)

MENU

FAMINE

INTRODUCTION ...

In a World in which we constantly hear of food mountains, and we make the choice of taking or not taking breakfast, it is difficult to appreciate that there exists a situation where millions of people are starving to death.

The record for going without food is held by nine Irishmen who were in Cork Gaol in 1920, and went on a hunger strike. They still lived after doing without food for 94 days (13 weeks and 3 days). They **chose** to do without food - but every day 10,000 people in Africa, India and South America starve to death. Two out of every three people in the World suffer from malnutrition.

In **LIMA**, Peru, a study done by the University of San Fernando showed that 93 out of every 100 children suffer from hunger, and only 2 out of the 100 get milk to drink each day. Also in Lima, half of the population live in slum dwellings of one room which lack drinking water and all hygienic services.

In **BOLIVIA**, you have reached a ripe old age if you survive until you are 45. That is about the same life expectancy as it was in England in the reign of Henry VIII. (- Unless, of course, you were one of his wives, then you were "axing" for trouble!)

Each day, human need stares at us from our televisions and from the pictures in the newspapers - but we still! go on buying bigger cars, new shoes, fancy haircuts, £25 perms. We don't even feel hungry. We seem to get our priorities all wrong. In **CALCUTTA**, lepers die in the gutters - yet we fit artificial hearts. We spend more on chewing gum a year than the Government gives in foreign aid.

THINGS GETTING WORSE

What we must realise is that things are not getting better - they are getting worse. The little lad begging for food in the Oxfam poster has now grown up, or died, and there are another twenty more bony bodies who need rice.

SOME FACTS ABOUT THE THIRD WORLD

O.H.P. 1   O.H.P. 2

FAMINE

RELEVANT QUOTATIONS ...

"The rich nations can be a force for tremendous good. When we die and appear before God, and He says: 'Did you feed them, did you give them to drink, did you clothe them, did you shelter them?' and we say, 'Sorry, Lord, but we did give them 0.3% of our gross national product', I don't think it will be enough!" (Barbara Ward)

"Since there are so many people in this World afflicted with hunger, this sacred Council urges all, both individuals and Governments, to remember the saying of the Fathers: 'Feed the man dying of hunger, because if you have not fed him, you have killed him!'" (Second Vatican Council - 'The Church Today')

CONCLUSION

The message is that we need to do, and give, a lot more. We cannot leave it all to Bob Geldof, Mother Teresa of Calcutta and the Save the Children Fund. We must give to all who need, and do whatever is possible to persuade others and Governments to give more and more.

PRAYER

Let us remember today all of those living in the Third World and elsewhere who are suffering through lack of food and through disease. Let us realise how lucky and how well off we are compared with so many others. We thank God for our homes, for sufficient food, for medical treatment, and for all of those amenities which make our lives so comfortable. Whenever we have the chance, let us give generously and unselfishly.

O.H.P. 3

MENU

FAMINE

SCRIPTURE READING

St. Mark, Chapter 6: verses 35-44 (The Feeding of the 5,000)

When it was getting late, His Disciples came to Him and said: "It is already very late, and this is a lonely place. Send the people away, and let them go to the nearby farms and villages in order to buy themselves something to eat."

"You yourselves give them something to eat," Jesus answered.

They asked: "Do you want us to go and spend two hundred silver coins on bread in order to feed them?"

So Jesus asked them: "How much bread have you got? Go and see."

When they found out, they told him: "Five loaves and also two fish."

Jesus then told His Disciples to make all the people divide into groups and sit on the green grass. So the people sat down in rows, in groups of a hundred and groups of fifty. Then Jesus took the five loaves and the two fish, looked up to Heaven, and gave thanks to God. He broke the loaves and gave them to His Disciples to distribute to the people. He also divided the two fish among them all. Everyone ate and had enough. Then the Disciples took up twelve baskets full of what was left of the bread and the fish. The number of men who were fed was five thousand.

MENU

FAMINE
MATERIAL FOR O.H.P.

O.H.P. 1

SOME FACTS ABOUT THE THIRD WORLD

- The **THIRD WORLD** has two-thirds of the World's population, but only produces 44% of the World's food
- One third of the World's people eat half of its food
- One quarter of the World's population are in need
- An estimated 500 million suffer from malnutrition
- Malnutrition and diarrhœa claim the lives of an estimated 15 million infants a year, and account for an average life expectancy of 48 years
- Water-related diseases claim 12 million infant lives annually
- In Britain there is, on average, one doctor per 1,800 people. In poor countries, there is one doctor for every 4,000.

O.H.P. 2

The despair of hunger

FAMINE
MATERIAL FOR O.H.P.
(Continued)

O.H.P. 3

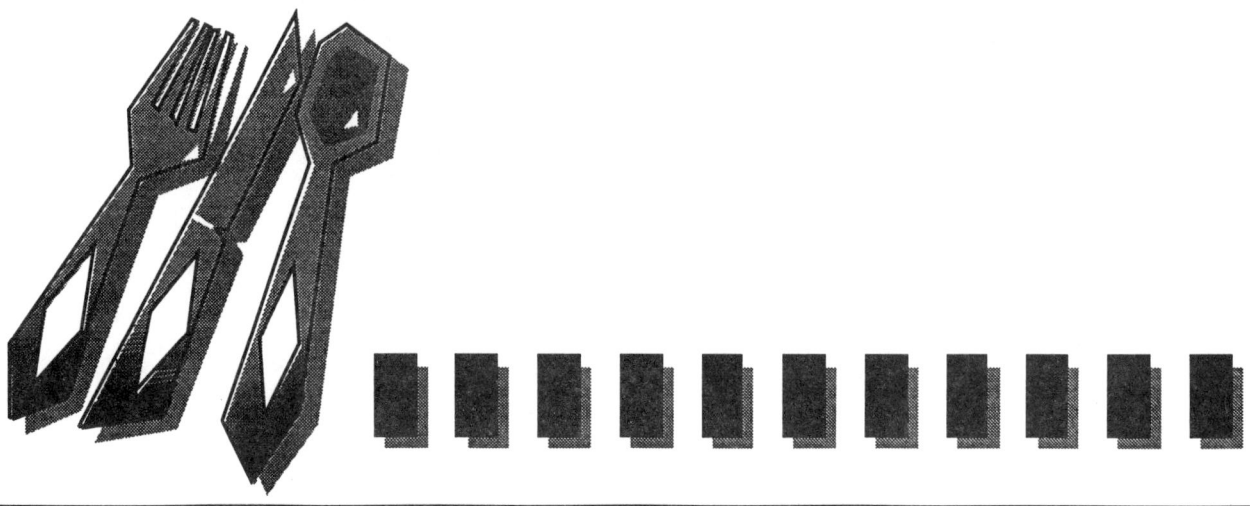

MENU

FAMINE

SUGGESTED RESOURCES ...

THE PICTURES
(OVERHEAD PROJECTOR)

- Facts about the Third World
- The Despair of Hunger
- Supermarket Shelves

THE MUSIC

- "Do They Know It's Christmas?" - Band Aid
- "From A Distance" - Nancy Quin
- "New World In The Morning" - Roger Whittaker
- "Water, Water" - Garth Hewitt
- "Road To Freedom" - Garth Hewitt
- "Record Of The Weak" - Garth Hewitt
- "Is This The World We Created?" - Queen

THE WORDS

SCRIPTURE READING

St. Mark, Chapter 6: verses 35-44
(The Feeding of the 5,000)

TALK AND GOSSIP

INTRODUCTION ...

The longest real word in the Oxford English Dictionary is:

O.H.P. 1   **FLOCCIPAUCINIHILIPILIFICATION**

and is defined as meaning "The action or habit of estimating as worthless." And so the next time you tell someone that they are useless, then you have been guilty of .... !

THE POWER OF WORDS

Words can generate all sorts of feelings, reactions and emotions. They are the most powerful weapons for good or evil that we have at our disposal. They are fundamental to all our relationships. They can ...

- ... make people **laugh**:   O.H.P. 2

    Two fish in a tank. The little one says to the big one: "Hey, do you know how to drive this thing?"

    or

    Two cows were grazing in a field, and one said to the other: "What do you make of this 'Mad Cows' disease'?" "I don't know," said the other. "I'm a duck!"   O.H.P. 3

- ... **gratify** and **gladden**:

    when the words "thank you", "sorry" or "please" are used.

- ... **encourage**:

    How often do individuals feel much better and try harder because someone has told them how well they are doing?

- ... bring **comfort** at times of great distress and bereavement:

    ("*Death is nothing at all ...*")   O.H.P. 4

- ... be **inspirational**:

    Probably the greatest, and certainly the best known, contribution made by Sir Winston Churchill during World War II was the encouragement and motivation he provided through his broadcasts to the nation during the bleakest hours. One of his most famous speeches in 1940, when it seemed Hitler's air force would win the Battle of Britain which would lead to an invasion of England, included the words:

    "We shall defend our island, whatever the cost may be. We shall fight on the beaches, we shall fight on the landing grounds, we shall fight in the fields and in the streets, we shall fight in the hills; we shall never surrender." (June, 1940)

    O.H.P. 5

TALK AND GOSSIP

However, words can also be extremely **destructive**. The popular saying: ***"Sticks and stones may break my bones, but words can never hurt me"*** is wrong and foolish. Far more accurate is an ancient Italian proverb which asserts: ***"The tongue has no bones, but it can break your back."***

It is well to understand that harsh and vicious words can destroy a person's life, and the most pernicious use of words is through gossip and the spreading of rumours.

AN OLD JEWISH STORY ...

Once there was a man who had a wife and four children and lived happily enough in a small town. He was content with life. He owned a pie shop which attracted many customers, because he always used the best meat and was skilled as a pastry cook. He was satisfied with making a reasonable profit as long as he could make ends meet and so the price of his pies were kept low. One day another man opened a pie-shop in the town, and a woman went in to ask how much the pies were. When she was told, she informed the owner that she would not buy them there because they were too expensive and she would continue to patronise the pie shop she had always used because she could obtain them for half the price. The new pie shop man told her that she would be unwise to do that because the pies being sold there were made of meat which had been condemned as unfit for human consumption.

The woman believed the man, bought his pies and began to spread the word that the pies in the other shop were dangerous to eat. The result was that, in time, no-one in the small town went to the long-established pie-man, and he was forced to close down. This was despite the fact that he had notices from the Food Inspectors displayed in his windows, saying that the meat used was perfectly good.

One day the new pie man was going to the synagogue, and there on the steps was the bankrupt pie-man with his wife and four children looking absolutely destitute and begging to obtain money for food. He was seized with guilt because he had been the cause of such misery. He went to the Rabbi and asked what he could do to feel better. The Rabbi told him to go home, go upstairs to his bedroom and take one of his feather pillows to the open window. There, with the pillow hanging outside, he should cut the pillow and and let the feathers fly into the air. He returned home and immediately did what the Rabbi had suggested. He then went back to the Rabbi and asked whether he had done enough.

"No", said the Rabbi. "What I want you to do now is to go and collect each feather which dropped out of the pillow."

"I'll never be able to do that", said the new pie man.

"No", said the Rabbi. "And that is what it is like when you spread rumours - true or false - about anyone. You can never retrieve them. They are like the feathers in the wind; they scatter everywhere, and affect everyone who comes into contact with them."

TALK AND GOSSIP

CONCLUSION

Gossip and rumours damage the person who spreads them, the people who listen to them and the person they concern. Once an individual has gossiped about someone or spread a story which will harm them, the relationship will never be the same again. A person may forget the hurt but never the pain caused. Where once there was trust now there will be distrust, where there was friendship there will be aversion and where there was loyalty, now there will be suspicion.

SCRIPTURE READING

St. Mark, Chapter 12: verses 28-31

A Teacher of the Law ... came to Him with a question: "Which Commandment is the most important of all?"

Jesus replied: "The most important one is this: 'Listen, Israel. The Lord our God is the only Lord. Love the Lord your God with all your heart, with all your soul, with all your mind, and with all your strength.' The second most important Commandment is this: 'Love your neighbour as you love yourself.' There is no other Commandment more important than these two."

ALTERNATIVE SCRIPTURE READING

Philippians, Chapter 2: verses 1-4

Your life in Christ makes you strong, and His love comforts you. You have fellowship with the Spirit, and you have kindness and compassion for one another. I urge you, then, to make me completely happy by having the same thoughts, sharing the same love, and being one in soul and mind. Don't do anything from selfish ambition or from a cheap desire to boast, but be humble towards one another, always considering others better than yourselves. And look out for one another's interests, not just for your own.

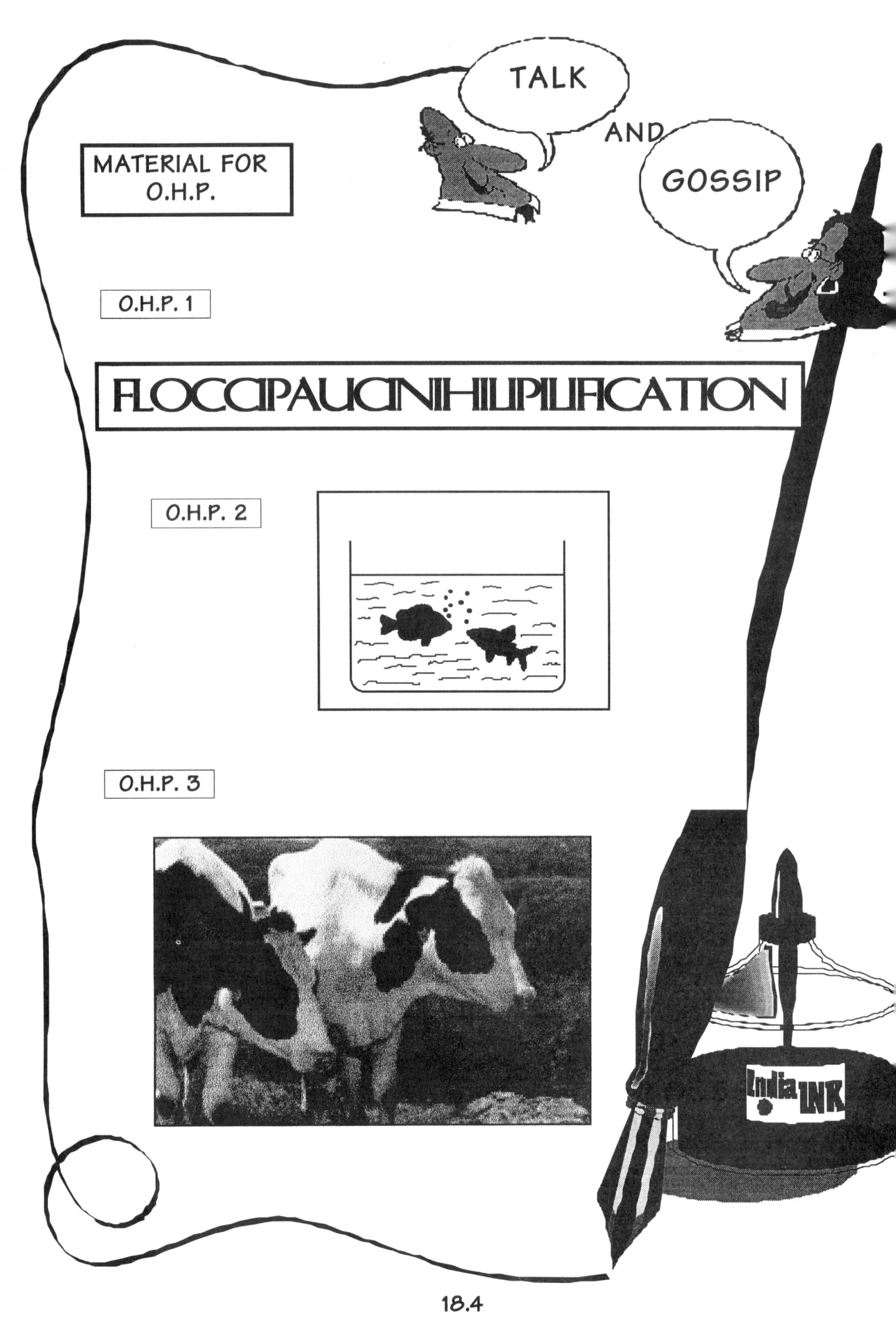

MATERIAL FOR O.H.P.
(Continued)

TALK AND GOSSIP

O.H.P. 4

"Death is nothing at all ... I have only slipped away into the next room ... I am I and you are you ... whatever we were to each other, that we are still. Call me by my own familiar name, speak to me in the easy way you always used to. Put no difference into your tone; wear no forced air of solemnity or sorrow. Laugh as we always laughed at the little jokes we enjoyed together. Play, smile, think of me, pray for me. Let my name be ever the household word that it always was. Let it be spoken without effect, without the ghost of a shadow on it. Life means all that it ever meant. It is the same as it ever was; there is absolutely unbroken continuity. What is death but a negligible accident? Why should I be put out of mind because I am out of sight? I am but waiting for you, for an interval, somewhere very near, just around the corner ... All is well."

O.H.P. 5

"WE SHALL DEFEND OUR ISLAND, WHATEVER THE COST MAY BE. WE SHALL FIGHT ON THE BEACHES, WE SHALL FIGHT ON THE LANDING GROUNDS, WE SHALL FIGHT IN THE FIELDS AND IN THE STREETS, WE SHALL FIGHT IN THE HILLS; WE SHALL NEVER SURRENDER."
(JUNE, 1940)

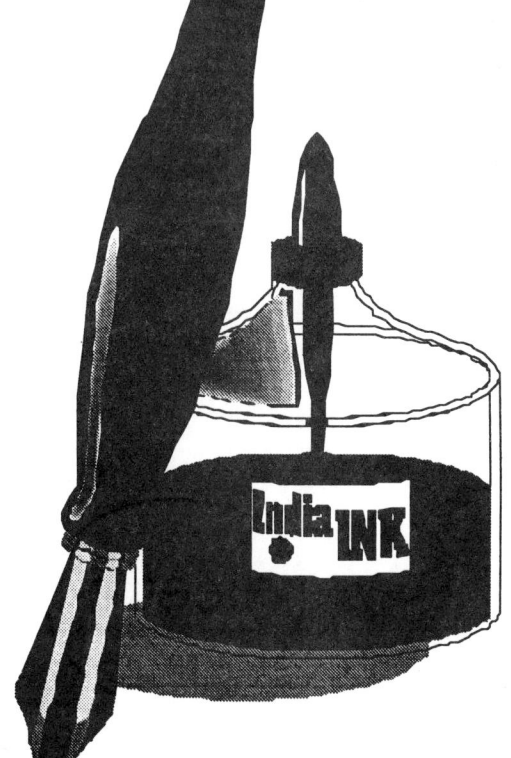

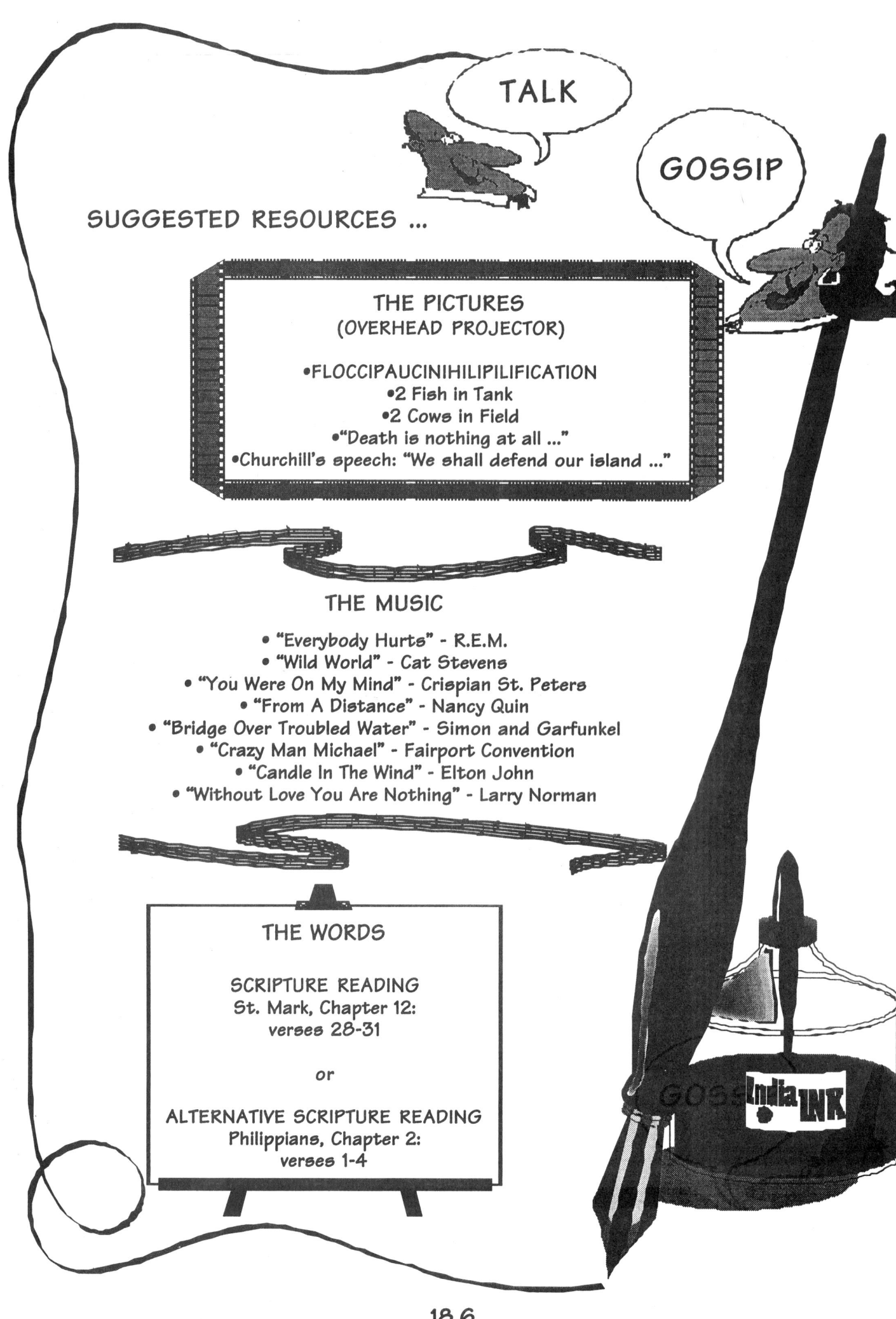

A NEW START

INTRODUCTION ...

New starters from Junior Schools experience a mixture of emotions on coming to the "big" school. They are excited at the prospect of entering a new phase in their lives, but a little wary because they are leaving a small establishment and coming into a much larger complex where the traditional folklore of initiation ceremonies has been gleefully handed down to them. Here is a tale to ease their worries.

FREDDY THE FROG

Once, in a far distant land, there was a little pond, not much bigger than the area in which we are today. And in the pond there were tadpoles who would flit in and out of the reeds and the pebbles which were in the shallow waters. Freddy was one of these tadpoles and he always used to be in the company of his elder brother, Franky. Eventually, they became healthy little frogs and really used to enjoy themselves playing "tig", hide and seek and having the odd game of water-head-football, using a lilac bud as a ball. They knew everybody, and everybody knew them, and they loved it.

One day, a cousin of theirs arrived whose name was Fritz, and who had travelled from a much bigger pond which he told them about. In fact, it was more of a lake than a pond, and it was only a short distance away. There, Fritz, told them, there was so much more to do - the bigger frogs taught the little ones how to do backward flips and somersaults, to play water-polo, water-skiing and all other sorts of games. Fritz described the delights so well that Franky, much to Freddy's disappointment, decided to return with him. Freddy still enjoyed himself with his friends, but he kept on wondering how Franky was getting on and what it was like in the Lake.

A NEW START

FREDDY THE FROG
(Continued)

A year went by, and Franky returned and persuaded Freddy he should go back with him to the Lake. He was very sad at leaving the little pond and he was worried about going to the Lake. All sorts of questions came into his head: Would it be so big he would get lost? Would he get bullied by the fish and the elder frogs? Would he make new friends? Would he be able to do all the new things? He was very excited at the prospect, but a little frightened. But, he knew that he had his elder brother, and there were old and wise frogs there who were only too ready to lend a hand and look after the young ones. So, off he hopped to the Lake.

It did take him a bit of time to get used to everything being so different, but it did not take him him long to settle in, and he loved the new experiences. Right from the start, he was determined to do as best he could and to enjoy himself - and because he did, he really enjoyed it. After a few weeks, he looked back on his little pond with affection, and while he would enjoy a visit there at some time in the future, he had no wish to return. Soon, he found himself going back to his little pond once a year, to let them know how much he enjoyed his new life and to tell them that they need not be concerned about the size, the many friends they would make, the many people who were there to help them, and the enjoyment they would have with all the new work.

CONCLUSION

The analogy between the "big" school and the Lake is obvious. Pupils can be assured that it will not take them long to settle in to their new routine and enjoy the variety and challenges of the different activities.

A NEW START

SUGGESTED RESOURCES ...

THE PICTURES
(OVERHEAD PROJECTOR)

Series of Scenes:
- Tadpoles in Pond
- Frogs Playing Together

THE MUSIC

- "We All Stand Together" - Paul McCartney
- "United We Stand" - Brotherhood of Man
- "The Voyage" - Christy Moore

CARE ON HOLIDAY

INTRODUCTION ...

Over the next few weeks, pupils will be commencing their holidays. It will be a change in routine where they escape temporarily the pressures, but also the security and the discipline which their schools afford. Inevitably, because they are under less supervision, with time on their hands, then they are more at risk. Certain activities and situations are more dangerous than others, and therefore special care needs to be taken.

Some things will constitute **no risk** for them, as they have for others. Take the case of the gluttonous Sylvanus "Hambone" Smith.

> *Sylvanus "Hambone" Smith III, who ate himself to death, was eventually buried in the Summer of 1995. Sylvanus, from Tiflon, Georgia, finally weighed in at 71 stone, having passed away owing to obesity. He had not been out of bed for two years, and his funeral had to be delayed while the 4' x 8' coffin, too big to go through the Church doors, was made. The service eventually took place in a warehouse, his coffin being carried to the cemetery on a specially reinforced truck.*

Nor are they likely to put themselves in danger in the way the "Motorway Vicar" did in April 1995, when he hurtled along the hard shoulder of the M6 at 5 m.p.h. in a two-wheeled vehicle for the disabled. Travelling from West Bromwich to Birmingham, he had decided such was the quickest route. After he had been escorted off the motorway, a Police Constable said: "This is certainly not advisable."

> Nor, some years ago, was it advisable for an Essex Granny to ride her bike the wrong way up the M25, looking for somewhere to buy a bottle of milk.

These dangers, which demonstrate at the very least a lack of awareness, fall into the risk category of "highly improbable", though not impossible. This next incident comes under the category of "highly unlikely", but possible.

O.H.P. 1

> In 1995, Levan Merritt, visiting Jersey Zoo and eagerly trying to improve his view, fell over the parapet into the Gorillas' compound. Alerted by the smaller gorillas, Jambo, the 40-stone leader, decided the boy was no threat, and protected him from the from his less sensitive colleagues. One gorilla was a particular threat, especially when Levan recovered consciousness and started to scream. Eventually Levan was rescued by the Zoo Keepers.

CARE ON HOLIDAY

The following activities and situations are those which constitute the greatest risk ...

O.H.P. 2

And then, by way of a light diversion, we have the danger always in our midst - man's best friend, the dog.

A Reporter, writing an article on Rottweilers and Bull Terriers, used the title: "TERRORISTS ON FOUR LEGS". He wrote this:

> "NEVER attempt to stare down a Rottweiler. When the animal - the black and tan terrorist of the dog world - is about to attack, he does so in silence, completely still, without growling or raising his hackles. The first warning may be an intimidating glare.
>
> "To stare back is to issue a challenge the dog is unlikely to ignore. Attack is the best, and possibly only, form of defence, according to Gavin Grant, a dog expert with the RSPCA.
>
> "Shout and try to dominate the dog by 'exuding power', he advises. Above all, don't run - unless you have somewhere to run to - and try not to show you are afraid, because the dog will sense it.
>
> "If this doesn't work, you have a serious problem."

O.H.P. 3

The question is - what *do* you do when you are confronted by a dog which has a clear desire to remove your right leg - or even worse!?

You certainly cannot take the declarations of the owners, who, after all, are the ones to blame for their dogs' behaviour, but who always have what to them must sound a plausible explanation:

- **It was because you were running!** (Fair comment, but now I have stopped, would you mind asking him to take his teeth out of my backside!)

- **He's just a puppy!** (Perhaps - but he's still built like a donkey.)

- **Strange - He's very good with children!** (That is nice to know - but I'm an old man.)

- **You'll be all right if you stand still and show no fear ...!** (I assure you I am motionless with terror!)

- **Are you a Foreigner?** (Unworthy of comment.)

- **He can smell your fear!** (Oh, if it were only fear!)

- **You have something he wants!** (Mrs. - he can have anything he wants as long as it is not part of my anatomy.)

- **If you could just stop shaking ...**

CARE ON HOLIDAY

However that which probably ruins so many holidays is the conflict and hassle which so often takes place when families are thrown together for a period which exceeds a week-end. It is such a pity that families look forward to holidays for so long, and so very often they are destroyed by selfishness and lack of consideration over what are frequently petty and paltry matters.

CONCLUSION

During holidays it might not be a bad idea for all of us to be *carefree*, *careful* and show *care* and kindness - AND still enjoy ourselves.

PRAYER FOR THE HOLIDAYS

Let us make a determined effort to make sure that, while we have a great break, we do not act in such a selfish and inconsiderate way that we ruin the holidays of our friends and families who might only have this one chance of having time off during the year.

Let us also be very conscious of all the dangers which surround us, and not put ourselves into hazardous situations.

We pray that we all return fit and well to commence the new Term.

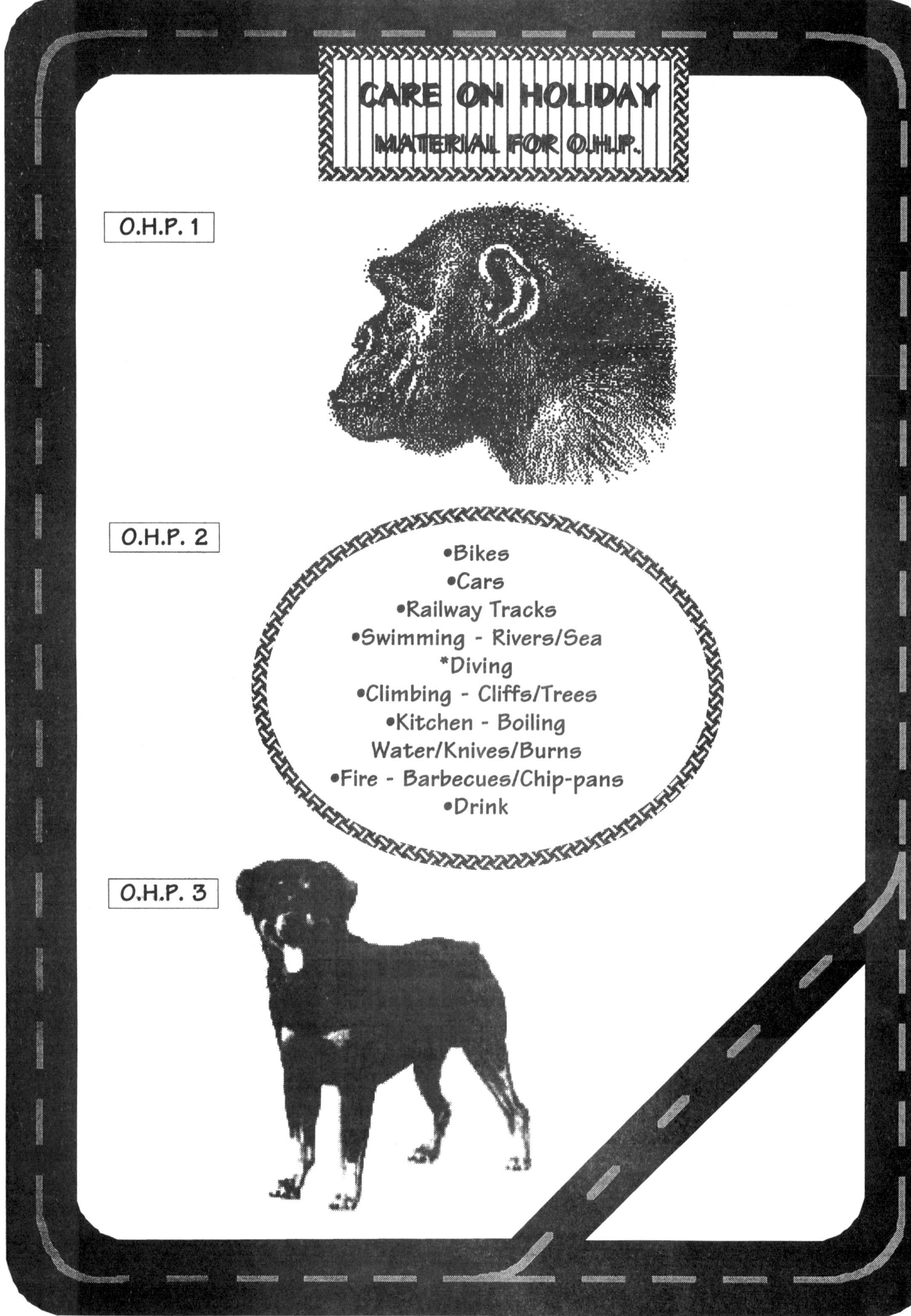

CARE ON HOLIDAY

SUGGESTED RESOURCES ...

THE PICTURES
(OVERHEAD PROJECTOR)

- Picture of Gorilla
- Dangers on Holiday
- Picture of Rottweiler

THE MUSIC

- "It's A Holi-Holiday" - Boney M
- "Summertime Blues" - Eddie Cochran
- "School's Out" - Alice Cooper
- "Thank You For The Days" - Kirsty MacColl

THE WORDS

A PRAYER FOR THE HOLIDAYS

ESSENTIAL ASSEMBLIES FOR ALL

Vol. II of **"Essential Assemblies for All"** is currently being compiled, with an estimated date for publication around Easter 1997.

If you would like the opportunity to place a priority order for a copy of Vol. II, please send your name and address to:

> **Vin Shanley**
> **CLARUS PUBLICATIONS**
> **51 Kader Avenue**
> **Acklam**
> **Middlesbrough**
> **Cleveland TS5 8NH**

and information will be sent to you as soon as it becomes available.

If, in the meantime, there are any comments or observations you would like to make concerning the content or format of Vol. I, or have any suggestions for Vol. II (for example, any specific themes you would like to see included), the author would be delighted to hear from you.

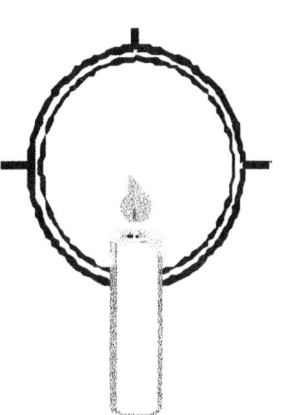

CLARUS PUBLICATIONS

51 Kader Avenue, Acklam, Middlesbrough, Cleveland TS5 8NH

Vin Shanley
February 1996